PATHWAYS IN PRODUCT

Mastering The Craft From Ideation To Implementation And Beyond

Andrei Adam

For Aspiring Product Professionals

Your compass to navigate the Product realm

Pathways in Product: Mastering the Craft From Ideation to Implementation and Beyond

Author: Andrei Adam

TABLE OF CONTENTS

Chapter One: Understanding the Landscape

Chapter Two: Product Strategy and Vision

Chapter Three: Getting Hands-On

Chapter Four: Collaboration and Stakeholder Management

Chapter Five: Inner Harmonies

Chapter Six: Becoming the Storyteller

Chapter Seven: Transitioning Into Product Roles

Chapter Eight: Final Thoughts

INTRODUCTION

*A*bout twelve years ago, one late afternoon, I found myself squatting on the floor after a very long day at the office, leaning against our old couch. My daughter, barely a year old at that time, reached up and started pulling at my suit. She wanted me to play with her, but I was miles away, lost in a haze. That piercing moment of disconnect still haunts me. It served as a jarring wake-up call, stressing the urgent need for change in my life.

It would be easy to point fingers at my banking career, thinking it wore me down. And for a while, I did. Because for a while, it had. But with time, I realised that those ten years were the very bedrock upon which I could build a new chapter.

My fascination with technology and my natural ability to connect with people made me think that perhaps I could transition into the role of a Business Analyst. However, the landscape was varied, and each company seemed to have its own vision of what a Business Analyst or Product Owner should be doing. I worried about being pigeonholed into a role that had me doing mundane tasks. Still, I took the plunge, spurred by my deep-seated need to change and do more. For myself and for my family. For my happiness. My wife was my unwavering anchor throughout this journey, grounding me whenever I veered off course, yet constantly offering her steadfast support and *encouragement.*

The career shift could have been smoother. It felt like navigating treacherous waters without a compass. Every day with new lessons, some tougher than others. Oh, how I wished for a guide, a roadmap to navigate this uncharted path. And how I wished I knew what I was getting into beforehand...

So, that's what I set out to create with this book.

Maybe you're in a place similar to where I was, contemplating a transition to the Product sphere. Or perhaps you've already taken the plunge and are seeking some anchor points. I've poured my journey, learnings, and heart into these pages. This isn't just a book about processes and tools. It's a dive into the daily life of a Product professional. It's about connections, it's about tailoring tech to real-world needs, and it's about constantly aiming to improve.

I hope this book provides some guidance, clarity, and maybe even a shortcut or two drawn from genuine experiences and insights. As you turn these pages, you'll find the essence of what it's like to traverse the dynamic landscape of Product, making decisions that matter and crafting solutions that make people's lives better. Dive in, relish every word, and take on the challenges and accomplishments that await in the Product world.

CHAPTER ONE

Understanding the landscape

I n the modern corporate world, there are many titles floating around, each of them marking different sets of responsibilities and levels of expertise. Among these, three roles within the product domain often seem to overlap and interweave: the Business Analyst (BA), the Product Owner (PO), and the Product Manager (PM). While these titles often become synonymous in conversation, they each offer unique values to a product's lifecycle. Let's decipher, differentiate, and appreciate the nuances of each.

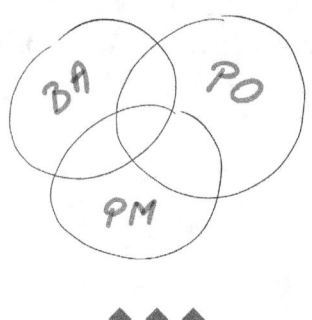

◆ ◆ ◆

The Triad Of The Product Realm

The Business Analyst (BA) is the bridge between business and technology. BAs dive deep into the processes, identifying and translating business needs into technical requirements. Their focus lies in rigorously analysing current processes and systems to pinpoint inefficiencies or areas of improvement. They meticulously document requirements, specifications, and processes, ensuring all stakeholders are on the same page. BAs also play a crucial role in validating that the implemented solutions indeed address the business needs they were designed to solve.

The Product Owner (PO) is the champion of the product's vision. They are the voice of the user, ensuring that the development team delivers maximum value. The PO is responsible for creating and prioritising the product backlog. This ever-evolving to-do list is central to Agile development. POs interact closely with stakeholders, assimilating feedback and aligning expectations. The PO makes on-the-spot decisions during the development cycle, ensuring the product remains true to its vision and objectives.

The Product Manager (PM) is the strategic force behind the product, overseeing its entire lifecycle, from inception to market launch and beyond. PMs set the long-term vision and strategy for the product. They often ask, "Where should our product be next year or five years from now?". They immerse themselves in market research, understanding competitors, and identifying market gaps. PMs work across teams, from sales and marketing to design and development, ensuring all the components of this machinery move synchronously towards the product's success.

At first glance, these roles might seem quite distinct. However, overlaps do exist. All three roles centre on delivering value: BAs ensure processes are optimised, POs prioritise features for immediate value, and PMs strategise for long-term product value. Both POs and PMs champion the user, though in different capacities. While POs prioritise immediate user needs in the backlog, PMs strategise on how to meet user needs in the broader market context. BAs and POs often collaborate closely with development teams. BAs translate business needs into technical requirements and POs are guiding the team through the development cycle.

While the Business Analyst, Product Owner, and Product Manager may wear different hats, they all converge on a shared mission: to create outstanding products that resonate with users and thrive in the market.

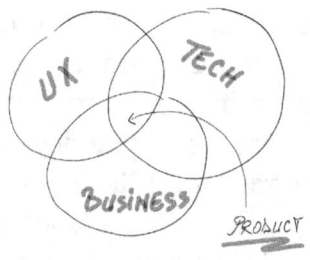

Understanding their roles is crucial for any organisation aiming for product excellence. This triad might seem like a complicated dance, but in reality, it's a harmonious ballet, with each role gracefully complementing the others in the grand performance of product creation.

◆ ◆ ◆

Comparisons And Overlaps

In-house Development vs Outsourcing

Understanding the roles is only half the battle. The context in which these roles operate also plays a key part in determining their responsibilities and interactions. Two dominant paradigms of product development, building in-house versus outsourcing, offer contrasting environments, affecting how our triad of roles (Business Analyst, Product Owner, and Product Manager) engage and collaborate.

In-house Product Development:

When a company crafts its own product, there's a deeply rooted sense of ownership across all levels. The BA, PO, and PM relationship is more integrated and often fluid here. The proximity, both physically and culturally, ensures that BAs, POs, and PMs can easily communicate, discuss concerns, align visions, and iterate quickly.

Everyone, from the top management to the development teams, shares a common understanding and commitment to the product's vision and objectives. The PM defines the overarching strategy, the PO ensures day-to-day tasks align with that strategy, and the BA bridges any technical or process-oriented gaps.

Quick feedback loops enable swift iterations. The PM can test a strategy, rely on the PO to implement it on the ground, and get feedback from the BA regarding potential business or technical challenges.

Outsourcing Model:

In outsourcing, product development occurs outside the company's walls, typically in a separate organisation or even a different country. The dynamics here become more layered. Given the contractual nature of outsourcing, roles often have more explicit boundaries.

The BA, usually part of the outsourcing team, spends significant time gathering detailed requirements to ensure clarity and reduce potential back-and-forth.

The PO becomes a crucial link between the in-house team and the outsourcing partner. They must clearly communicate the product's vision and priorities to the external team, ensuring that the outsourced development aligns with the company's objectives.

The PM assumes a more strategic and supervisory role in this model. They focus on the bigger picture, market trends, and overarching product goals, relying heavily on the PO to translate this vision effectively to the outsourcing partner.

Still, there is synergy across models. The BA, PO, and PM are integral parts of the product development machine in both models. While in-house development offers more organic and immediate collaboration, outsourcing requires defined boundaries and more precise delineations of responsibility.

Yet, in either scenario, their collective aim remains unchanged: delivering a product that resonates with its users and achieves its business objectives.

Product vs Project Management

To fully grasp the convergence and divergence between Product roles (Business Analyst, Product Owner, and Product Manager) and that of the Project Manager, it's vital to understand the lineage, the present-day interplay, and the misconceptions that often blur the boundaries between these crucial roles.

Rooted in the early marketing principles from the mid-20th century, product management emerged to champion the voice of the customer within a company. Initially focused on tangible goods, its reach expanded with the digital revolution. As software and online services bloomed, the roles of Product Manager, Product Owner, and Business Analyst crystallised, each addressing distinct facets of product creation and enhancement.

Project Management, on the other hand, predates its product-focused counterpart, tracing back to monumental endeavours like the Pyramids or the Great Chinese Wall. The modern concept, however, solidified in the 20th century, particularly with the rise of large-scale automotive, construction, defence, and aerospace projects. The Project Management Institute (PMI) further formalised the discipline in the 1960s.

In today's digitally-driven landscape, both realms converge more than ever. With Agile methodologies championing a collaborative environment, Product and Project Managers often find themselves in joint ceremonies, from sprint plannings to retrospectives. The BA's requirements, the PO's user stories, and the PM's strategy all find their place within the Project Manager's timeline. Tools like Jira, Confluence, Trello, Asana, Miro and so on allow for a blending of product and project functions, further intertwining the roles. While a Product professional might be using these tools to prioritise features, for example, a Project Manager might employ them to track timelines and resource allocation.

At its core, product management is about the *what* and the *why*. It emphasises user needs, market trends, and business objectives. Project management, on the other hand, zeroes in on the *how* and the *when*, concentrating on timelines, resources, and deliverables. Product roles tend to have a lifecycle perspective. They see products as evolving entities that grow, change, and adapt. Project Managers operate within set start and end dates, driving projects to successful and timely conclusions. While both roles engage with stakeholders, they do so differently. Product roles frequently interface with end-users, sales teams, customer support and business executives to shape the product. In contrast, Project Managers often communicate with internal teams, ensuring resources are allocated, risks mitigated, and timelines met.

The mixture between product and project management stems from several different factors. With terms like "product lifecycle" and "project lifecycle" often used interchangeably, it's no wonder there's confusion. Both roles require exceptional communication, leadership, and organisational skills. This similarity often masks their distinct responsibilities. Last but not least, in startups or smaller teams, one might find a Product person also taking on project management duties (and vice versa), leading to blurred lines.

The Evolution Of Product Roles

The rapid technological shifts, including the surge in artificial intelligence, machine learning, and digitalisation, are undeniably shaping every corner of our lives, and the roles within product development are no exception.

Product Managers, Product Owners, and Business Analysts are becoming increasingly dependent on data-driven insights. AI, with its capability to analyse vast sets of data rapidly, will soon become their best ally. Instead of merely suggesting features based on intuition or limited user feedback, these professionals will have the power of predictive analytics and user behaviour models to forecast which features or changes would be most beneficial.

Routine tasks such as tracking minor bugs, understanding essential user feedback, or even backlog prioritisation can be streamlined with AI. This automation will allow Product roles to focus on more strategic, high-value tasks, emphasising creativity, strategy, and vision.

As user needs become more complex and demand hyper-personalization, the role of a Product Manager or Owner will pivot towards understanding nuances and crafting experiences that AI may very well suggest. AI can process and analyse user data, but human touch will be imperative to align technological capabilities with emotional intelligence and cultural nuances.

With technology advancing at such an incredible speed, Product roles must be perpetual students. Their roles will evolve into ones that can quickly adapt to new tools, understand AI recommendations, and ensure that products stay both technologically advanced and user-friendly.

As AI integration becomes more profound, ethical considerations will emerge. Product roles might evolve to become guardians of ethical product development, ensuring AI integrates into products in transparent, fair ways that don't compromise user privacy.

The Longevity of Product Roles in an Automated World

While it's tempting to think that machines might render human roles obsolete, several factors advocate the continued importance of humans in Product roles.

Machines lack the deep emotional understanding that humans possess. Crafting user experiences requires empathy, a grasp of cultural nuances, and an understanding of human behaviours in ways that go beyond algorithms. Human judgment will also be vital in making decisions that align with the values and norms of society. And while AI can provide data and even predictions, the creative process of brainstorming, conceptualising a vision for the product, and devising strategies to realise that vision requires a human touch. Not to mention that Product roles frequently liaise with diverse teams, from marketing to engineering. Such collaboration requires communication skills, negotiation, and an understanding of human dynamics that AI cannot replicate.

AI will undoubtedly become an invaluable tool in the product development arsenal. However, it will augment human capabilities rather than replace them. The fusion of human intuition, creativity, and emotional intelligence with AI's data-driven insights promises an exciting, innovative future for Product roles. The essence of these roles isn't just in the tasks they perform but in the human-centric value they bring, making them irreplaceable for the foreseeable future.

From the Trenches

Throughout my career, I've assumed many covers. I've been the meticulous Business Analyst, the visionary Product Owner, the driving force of a Product Manager, and countless other roles that defy simplistic labels. From the nimble dynamics of startups to the tangled corridors of multinational behemoths, my journey has cut across industries, from the algorithm-driven world of fintech to the life-saving arena of pharma, from the adrenaline of sports to the calculative play of betting, and from the immediacy of food delivery to the foundational realm of education.

Yet, regardless of the industry, the size of the company, or the nature of the project, there's a familiar pattern I've encountered time and again. The initial scepticism, the arched eyebrows, the questioning looks, and sometimes even the candid questions: "Why should you be on the billing sheet?" It's as though the value a Product role brings is an enigma wrapped in the financial documents.

And then, as the project moves from its early stages to full-blown execution, the very sceptics become enthusiastic fans. I've seen it happen too many times to count. Once they see the value, the meticulous planning, the bridge-building, and the strategic foresight, there's a newfound respect. Often, it's more than that; it's sheer reliance. And when it's time to move on and steer away towards a new project, the very client who once questioned my role becomes the one weeping its conclusion.

Another perennial challenge? The Product versus Project Manager debate. It's a conversation I've had more times than I care to remember. While both roles have their distinct significance, the lines often blur for those not knee-deep in the industry's intricacies.

Yet another recurring theme is the resistance to change, the allegiance to "this is how we've always done it". It's a feeling that's not unique to any particular industry. Humans, by nature, resist change, especially when it disrupts a familiar routine. But clinging to outdated methodologies is like holding onto an old map in a changed landscape. While the past offers lessons, it shouldn't become a crutch that prevents progress.

So, after countless projects, challenges, and innumerable conversations, what advice can I share? Approach every project with both an open heart and an open mind. Resistance is part of any change, and as someone at the forefront of product strategy, you're often the messanger of that change. Embrace the role. Educate, elucidate, and engage. Sometimes, it requires patience to explain intricate concepts as simply as to a child, often more than once. But remember, understanding breeds alignment. And always, always be ready to take that crucial first step toward collaboration. More often than not, it's you who has to bridge the gap. But that bridge, once built, paves the way for synchronicity, innovation, and success.

Always remember that pressure-packed situations often arise from a series of (unfortunate) choices. But choices, by their very nature, can be changed. So, when faced with challenges, do lean in, communicate, and lead the way. The path to harmonious collaboration and breakthrough innovations is often just one courageous conversation away.

◆ ◆ ◆

CHAPTER TWO

Product strategy and vision

◆ ◆ ◆

There's often a craving for simplicity in a world rampant with complexity. We need a handbook, a straightforward map labelled with a "5 steps to success" mantra. Yet, the wisdom we seek is often within us, nestled beneath piles of knowledge and experiences. However, the biggest challenge is to declutter and rearrange these insights into a cohesive pattern that illuminates our path.

◆ ◆ ◆

Innovation With A Human Touch

Introducing the buzzword of contemporary innovation: Design Thinking.

Design Thinking isn't a simple process. It's a philosophy, a mindset, and an operational blueprint that helps sculpt ideas into tangible, viable products. But what is it that sets Design Thinking apart? Why is it (still) gaining traction in today's dynamic landscape?

Dating back to the 1960s, Design Thinking emerged as a blend of imaginative techniques and systematic design methods. It borrowed principles like divergence, where a multitude of possible solutions are explored, and convergence, where those solutions are narrowed down. It championed the practice of prototyping, iterating, and validating ideas while emphasising sustainable solutions that could stand the test of time.

However, the true essence of Design Thinking lies in its "human-centred" approach. While traditional product development might prioritise usability, streamlined flows, and user-friendly interfaces, Design Thinking goes deeper. It taps into the realm of human emotions, digging deep to understand end users' desires, needs, and feelings. Beyond simply providing functional solutions, it aims to deliver experiences packed with added value.

You might ask, "Isn't that the same as a customer-centric approach?" Not quite. While a customer-centric mindset focuses on optimising the user experience from a usability standpoint, Design Thinking delves into the very psyche of the user. It's not just about making a product easy to use. It's about resonating with the user's innermost desires and needs. It's about crafting products that serve a purpose, evoke emotions, and foster connections.

Let's illustrate this with a simple example. Imagine you're designing a digital reading app. A customer-centric approach might prioritise features like customisable fonts, a night mode, and bookmarking capabilities. Design Thinking, on the other hand, would ask: "How does the user feel when they read? What emotions do they associate with reading? What atmosphere do they prefer?" Perhaps the app could simulate the scent of fresh pages or replicate the sound of turning a page, offering an experience beyond sheer reading; it provides the warmth and nostalgia of holding a physical book.

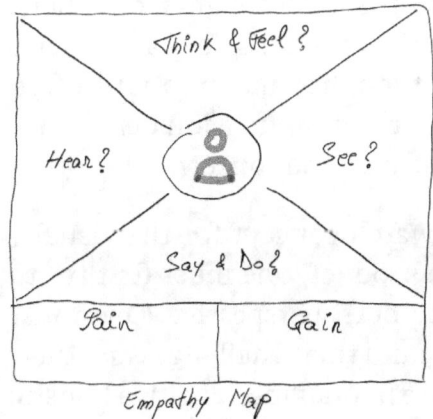

Empathy Map

The power of Design Thinking lies in its flexibility. While its roots are firmly planted in the design world, its principles are universal, transcending industries and domains.

To fully leverage the potential of Design Thinking, one doesn't need to be a designer by profession. Instead, one must adopt a designer's mindset, which is essentially an open, curious, empathetic, and solution-oriented way of viewing the world.

As we navigate modern-day challenges, Design Thinking guides us to create products and craft experiences. It reminds us that at the heart of every innovation lies a human being with emotions, desires, and dreams. And when we design with these humans in mind, we pave the way for solutions that are both efficient and deeply meaningful.

◆ ◆ ◆

The Quintessence of Design Thinking

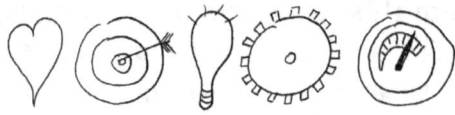

Every groundbreaking innovation begins with understanding. And at the core of understanding is empathy. Empathy isn't only about sympathising; it is a profound, immersive process, a conscious endeavour to dive deep into another person's experiences, emotions, and aspirations.

Empathy is an art, the ability to transcend our perspectives and truly resonate with the feelings and thoughts of others. While actions and words are the markers of a person's state, understanding their deeper thoughts and emotions often requires a nuanced lens. This level of comprehension demands a heightened sense of observation and genuine concern.

Take, for example, the smartwatch concept for the visually impaired. To craft a truly valuable product, one must first try to visualise the world from the customers' perspective. One must step into their daily life and understand their challenges and their deepest needs. It isn't just an exercise in imagination; it's a holistic dive into empathy.

Following this empathetic journey, we step into the realm of definition. This phase is similar to assembling a puzzle. Armed with insights from our empathetic exploration, we start organising, analysing, and synthesising the information. The objective? Pinpointing the specific challenges to address and devise potential solutions.

Defining isn't just about listing problems. It's a meticulous process of understanding causality, discerning implications, and highlighting challenges. Articulating problems is instrumental because it ensures clarity and is a testament to our comprehensive understanding.

The subsequent phase, ideation, is a wild explosion of creativity. Think of it as a brainstorming session on steroids. Every idea, no matter how wild or unconventional, is welcomed. Now is not the time for filters or judgments. It's an arena for unbridled innovation, where quantity truly trumps quality. Building upon others' ideas, venturing into uncharted territories, and visualising diverse solutions are the hallmarks of this phase.

As the storm of creativity settles, we transition into prototyping. Here, ideas metamorphose into tangible entities. However, these aren't superb, finished products but rather rudimentary versions. These prototypes serve a singular purpose: to test the feasibility and effectiveness of the chosen solutions in a real-world context. Iteration is the name of the game, with each version refined based on feedback, culminating in a prototype that encapsulates the optimal solution.

Finally, we arrive at the testing phase, a rigorous, exhaustive evaluation of the entire product. It is an intensive process that scrutinises every facet of the product, measuring its alignment with the identified solution.

But the essence of design thinking is its iterative nature. Testing isn't the grand finale. It is a feedback loop. Each test conveys further insights about the users, producing new ideas and occasionally encouraging a reevaluation of the problem statement.

Design thinking is a cyclical process. It doesn't end with one or a series of successful tests. Each iteration is a step closer to perfection, a move towards crafting products that aren't just functional but profoundly impactful.

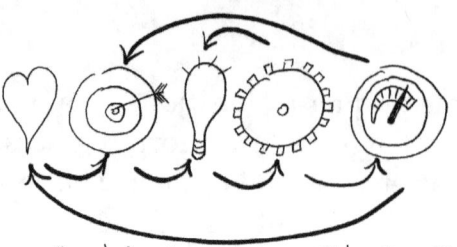

Empathize. Define. Ideate. Prototype. Test. REPEAT.

Design thinking is essentially more than just a five-step ladder to product perfection. It's a dynamic dance of empathy, creativity, and rigorous evaluation. It's a commitment to crafting solutions that resonate deeply with users, melding innovation with profound human understanding. Design thinking is a philosophy that places the user at the heart of every innovation.

The Product Vision

"The future belongs to those who believe in the beauty of their dreams." - Eleanor Roosevelt.

In product development, the vision is the North Star. It guides every decision, propels teams forward, and sets the course for the future. Crafting a compelling product vision is more than just a one-time activity. It's a commitment to understanding and articulating the very essence of a product's purpose. Furthermore, as markets shift and users evolve, so too must the vision, constantly adapting and refining to stay relevant and inspiring.

Before diving into the art of crafting a vision, it's essential to understand its fundamental components:

- *Purpose*: Why does this product exist? What change or value does it aim to bring into the world?
- *Target Audience*: Whom is the product intended for? What are their needs, aspirations, and challenges?
- *Differentiation*: How will the product stand out in the crowded marketplace? What makes it unique?

When crafting your vision, start with a blank canvas. Remember not to let past conventions or current assumptions box in your thinking. Beginning with a fresh perspective allows for genuine innovation. Engage multiple perspectives. Whether it's a brainstorming session with the team, feedback from potential users, or insights from industry experts, various viewpoints can offer invaluable insights.

Visualise the future. Imagine the world where your product exists. How has it changed the lives of its users? What broader implications does it have on society? Stay authentic. It's tempting to craft a vision that sounds grand, but authenticity is critical. Your product vision should resonate deeply with the company's values and beliefs.

The marketplace and user needs are in constant flux. A vision that doesn't adapt runs the risk of becoming obsolete. This evolution should be both proactive, anticipating future changes, and reactive, responding to unforeseen shifts.

However, there are many ways to tackle these challenges. Like scheduling periodic reviews of the product vision. Is it still aligned with the company's broader goals? Does it resonate with the current user base? Always keep communication channels with stakeholders open. Their feedback can provide critical insights into how the product vision might need to adjust. The world outside, be it technological advancements, societal shifts, or market dynamics, can influence the direction of your product. By staying informed, we can ensure the product vision remains relevant and future-facing.

It's a delicate balance. While adaptability is essential, a vision that shifts too often can lead to confusion and a lack of direction. The key is to remain consistent in the core principles and values while allowing flexibility in how they are interpreted and manifested.

A vision, no matter how compelling, loses its value if it doesn't drive action. Every decision, from feature prioritisation to marketing strategies, should align with and advance the product vision.

Crafting and evolving a product vision is not a destination but a continuous journey. It requires constant nurturing, reflection, and adaptation. But, when done right, it serves as the guiding light, illuminating the path to success and ensuring every step taken is purposeful and aligned.

A compelling product vision is more than just a statement; it is the soul of the product. It captures its essence, defines its trajectory, and inspires those who work on it. As the marketplace becomes increasingly dynamic, the importance of a robust and adaptable vision becomes essential. By crafting a vision rooted in genuine understanding and ensuring it evolves with the times, product leaders can set the stage for lasting success, impact, and legacy.

"However beautiful the strategy, you should occasionally look at the results." - Winston Churchill.

And "occasionally" is an understatement. In today's dynamic business environment, achieving alignment between company strategy and market objectives is equivalent to a maestro, ensuring every instrument in the orchestra plays in harmony. It is about choreographing a dance where each step complements the other, ensuring that the business not only survives but thrives in the ever-changing marketplace.

At its core, alignment is about cohesiveness. It ensures that internal strategies resonate with external market demands. The internal strategy encompasses the company's goals, culture, resources, and core competencies, while the market objectives include current market demands, foreseeable trends, competitor actions, and emerging technologies.

◆ ◆ ◆

Crafting A Cohesive Strategy

Start with introspection. What are the company's strengths, values, and aspirations? Identifying these creates a strong foundation. On the other hand, continuous research into market trends, customer preferences, and competitive landscapes helps align strategies with real-world demands. Then we must keep in mind that alignment isn't just a top-down approach. We need to engage various departments, from R&D to marketing, ensuring everyone is on the same page and contributing their insights.

When it comes to navigating market dynamics, remember that the marketplace is fluid. Companies that foresee changes and shift their strategies accordingly have a competitive advantage. With that in mind, we must employ systems that provide timely feedback from the market. This could be through customer surveys, beta testing, or monitoring social media reactions. Achieving market objectives is often more than a solitary journey. Collaborate with partners, vendors, and even customers to co-create value.

It's not uncommon for discrepancies to emerge between a company's strategic intent and market realities. Addressing these swiftly and decisively is crucial. Performing periodic reviews can identify potential misalignments early, enabling corrective action while encouraging a culture where teams can openly discuss challenges that will harbour insight-sharing without fear of retribution.

An aligned strategy is only as good as the results it produces. Regularly measure the outcomes, analyse them in the context of market objectives, and refine your approach. Establish clear KPIs reflecting company and market objectives. These serve as tangible markers of alignment and success. Recognise that alignment is an ongoing process. Learn from both successes and missteps and iteratively refine your strategies.

Beyond immediate business success, a well-aligned strategy boosts employee morale and engagement, fosters innovation, and enhances stakeholder trust. It creates a resonance where the company not only meets market needs but often anticipates and shapes them, establishing itself as a market leader.

Therefore aligning strategy with company and market objectives is both an art and a science. It's about syncing the company's aspirations and heartbeats with the market's pulse. Such alignment ensures the company remains relevant, resilient, and ready to seize opportunities, crafting a narrative of sustained growth and impactful presence in the marketplace.

Goals And Okrs

"A dream written down with a date becomes a goal. A goal broken down into steps becomes a plan. A plan backed by actions makes your dreams come true." Greg Reid.

For a bit of history, "MBOs" or "Management by Objectives" were the brainchild of Peter Drucker. Based on MBOs, Andy Grove then developed the basis of the OKR theory at Intel. This theory was then taught to John Doerr by Andy Grove. Doerr was the one who actually crafted the name "OKR". Doerr introduced the OKR philosophy to Google's founders in 1999, and OKRs (objectives and key results) have been used ever since, and an entire world started using them. Nobody says they are perfect. But so far, they have proved to be the best way to steer our ships.

Why is it so hard for us to define our goals? A goal, at the end of the day, is something that we want to do or achieve. And we usually do know what we want, but when someone asks us to phrase it as a goal, it's just as if it suddenly becomes real. If I say that I want to get a certification, it sounds like something that I'd be talking to my friends about. But if I say that my goal for next year, by the end of Q4, is to get certified as a Product Owner, well, that's a totally different story. It sounds official, and it becomes a burden.

Maybe that's what we could improve. Changing our mindset when it comes to goal setting and looking at it from a different angle. Acknowledging the fact that this is something that we're doing for our own benefit, it might change our perspective. Having a North Star, something to pursue, is always an excellent way to ensure we're heading in the right direction. Constantly monitoring our progress against the goals we've set for ourselves will keep us true to our course and immediately flag any detours.

Setting the right goals is of utmost importance. And so is their size. If your goals are too low, hence allowing you to easily accomplish them, that doesn't bring much value.

When it comes to goals, don't be afraid to raise the bar too high. Aim for the moon to land among the stars; that should be your motto. Don't be disappointed if you haven't touched the 100% milestone; be happy you've fulfilled half of it. It will most definitely be more than what you would have achieved by setting the bar too low for yourself.

Your goals have to be meaningful. They need to have a sense of purpose and serve as an inspiration. And just as John Doerr described in one of his TED talks, goals are "a kind of vaccine against fuzzy thinking".

The words "goals" and "objectives" are often confusing in the same sentence. But the truth is that they answer different questions, and when it comes to goals, the question we need to ask ourselves is "Why?". What drives us, what is our true motivation, why do we really want to do this? It has to do with our passion, with our feelings.

This is exactly why our goals need to be audacious, even outrageous! Goals are the lead vocalist in our band, the most prominent voice, the one that inspires, lifts up the spirit and provides guidance. And they do that by appealing to our feelings, to our dreams, to our beliefs.

In his war against poverty and disease, Bono has been using OKRs for years in his "ONE" global movement campaign, and the most accurate representation of his beliefs are Bono's actual words:

"So you're passionate? How passionate? What actions does

your passion lead you to do? If the heart doesn't find a perfect rhyme with the head, then your passion means nothing. The OKR framework cultivates the madness, the chemistry contained inside it. It gives us an environment for risk for trust, where failing is not a fireable offence. And when you have that sort of structure and environment and the right people, magic is around the corner."

From passion, your goals are brought to life. And when reason tunes in, OKRs are shaping up. Together, they provide the most comprehensive set of instructions for a higher purpose, for a unified and directional approach.

And on the same note, the statement of the "ONE" organisation sounds like this:

"ONE is a global movement campaigning to end extreme poverty and preventable disease by 2030 so that everyone, everywhere, can lead a life of dignity and opportunity. We believe the fight against poverty isn't about charity but about justice and equality."

Let's do a bit of analysis: the goal, the answer to "why?" is, in fact, the fight for justice and equality. The OKR, as stated above, is to end extreme poverty and preventable disease by 2030. We've got right here a prime example, one that follows all the rules: their goal is significant, concrete, action-oriented and inspirational. Their OKR is specific and time-bound, aggressive yet realistic, measurable and verifiable. And most importantly, their goal is supported by their OKR.

Now that we have spoken about setting up our goals, let's dive a bit into how to best achieve them. In one of his many chunks of wisdom, Simon Sinek formulates a very decent approach to achieving our goals. In his opinion, there are two different types of people in the world, people who envision their goal, and that's the only thing that they're focusing on, and there are people who can only see the blockages along the way, things that prevent them from achieving their goal. But you mustn't necessarily go in a straight line. You can bend the rules. The only thing that you must pay attention to is not to get in someone else's way when bending those rules, hence preventing them from achieving their own goals. This may come at a cost, you may need to compromise, but it will get you closer to your goals.

Another important aspect worth mentioning here is that we need to be careful not to become our own victims when articulating our goals. Something that I've seen in organisations throughout the years is that people have the tendency to formulate goals and objectives starting from what they've already got planned. In fact, they end up mapping their existing roadmap to their goals in a deceitful attempt to match the two. The result is a forced relationship, a completely unhealthy approach that changes nothing. You've got some goals written on a piece of paper, but you're going to do whatever you were going to do, anyway. That's a pretty straightforward recipe for failure.

You need to start fresh. A clean slate that should be your starting ground. Get rid of all the burdens generated by historical endeavours. Shake off that attachment to any previously set targets and milestones. Change your mindset and embrace the unknown, allowing yourself to rethink and reshape your future. That's how you've been doing it for decades? Well, guess what... The years have passed, and the world around you is not the same anymore. How else can you keep up, other than reframing and lifting the anchor that holds you grounded to a past that should act as a mentor, not as a drawback.

"If you commit to nothing, you'll be distracted by everything." the Tendai Buddhist monks.

Commitment and focus that's what we need. If we have a goal, then we've already begun setting the stage for our next steps. We've already defined our Objectives and our Key Results, and that's a clear statement of our commitment. Next, we need to figure out what exactly is it that we need to do in order to meet our objectives. Whatever we identify and define at this stage will actually turn into our high-level requirements. This will serve as our baseline when transitioning to the more tactical aspects later on.

Let me give you an example just to make sure that we're on the same page. One of the clients that I've worked with in the past they were facing this particular problem. Nothing unheard of, just that it was a thorn in their side, and they decided to act on it.

So here's the problem statement: customers were calling customer support at a high rate. This was, of course, time-consuming, and in time it became quite a money pit.

One of their strategic goals for that year was to reduce costs. And yes, before you ask, you can indeed have goals set in multiple strategic directions. And no, not all of the goals that companies set for themselves are about fighting for justice and equality.

So this particular problem was identified as a good match when ideating on how to achieve the previously mentioned goal. Given the context, the following OKR was then defined: the number of customer calls would need to be reduced by 20% within the next six months.

We had so far a goal and an OKR to guide us towards the goal. But the next question was: what is it that we can actually do to reduce the number of calls? And one of the answers was to improve the usability of confusing features. This became one of the high-level requirements.

What features to improve, how exactly could they be improved, what should the design look like, what should be changed in terms of user experience and why? All of these questions and a lot more are part of what a Product manager needs to figure out in order to define the requirement because you can't go to the development team and tell them to "improve the confusing features"; you need to approach them with a clear solution that will subsequently be implemented.

The good news is that the Product people don't do all of these by themselves; it's not a one-man show; it's a team effort. Many various capabilities need to be involved, and experts from multiple disciplines must contribute. You've got customer support, financial, marketing, sales, UX, technical experts, and so on. Everyone joins the effort so that a proper solution may be articulated.

I mentioned focus a bit earlier. It is of utmost importance to focus on one stage at a time. Otherwise, our brains will try to think of everything at once, with no proper outcome. When you are trying to dig out problems, do just that. Don't also think about how to solve those problems. When you're trying to generate ideas, and potential solutions for previously identified problems, do just that. Don't also try to think about how good or bad one idea is in particular. You'll have plenty of time for that in the next stage. For now, focus on volumes. Generate as many ideas as possible. At this point, you're interested in quantity, not quality. Once you've drained out all ideas, then you can focus on analysing them, triaging, categorising, prioritising and selecting the most suitable candidate to be used moving forward.

◆ ◆ ◆

The Illusion of Multitasking

I believe it's pretty obvious by now the reason why focusing on one thing at a time is extremely important to get optimal results. Besides the fact that creativity is stimulated when having such an approach, we're also managing our resources more wisely.

Guy Winch, PhD, author of "Emotional First Aid: Practical Strategies for Treating Failure, Rejection, Guilt and Other Everyday Psychological Injuries", explains why multitasking is a myth.

It has been demonstrated that we don't actually do five things at the same time. What our brain does, in fact, is switch extremely fast from one task to another. So if you're sitting at your desk reading an email while speaking with somebody from Financial on the phone and crunching some numbers based on that email while also eating your lunch and on top of all that, your monkey brain can't stop searching for a dinner recipe... Well, that couldn't be much farther from the truth! Take a deep breath, think about those processes in sequence, analyse them in slow motion, and I guarantee you that even without a PhD, you'll still get to the same conclusion.

Not to mention the fact that our brain is a champion when it comes to energy consumption at an industrial scale. That's why 5 minutes after that call with Financial, you'll get a headache, cramps, and an impossible weight on your eyelids, all at the same time. Because of all that "multitasking" draining you down.

This is why focus is so important. This is why tackling things one at a time is much more efficient, not to mention healthier for our bodies.

◆ ◆ ◆

From the Trenches

In the business world, where buzzwords like "strategy" and "vision" fly around like elusive butterflies, it's easy to misinterpret their significance. To some, they might appear as the garb of the C-suite, conjuring images of boardroom discussions and high-level decisions. But in the heart of the digital landscape, for Product Professionals, they are the essence, the soul, the very compass by which we navigate.

Imagine the daunting title of a "Digital Strategist." While it may sound grand, it fundamentally entails delivering a coherent digital strategy, a roadmap that charts our course, complete with well-defined goals and quantifiable metrics like OKRs.

However, the real challenge, and perhaps the true essence of a Product Professional's role, often lies beneath the surface. I recall my time with a well-funded startup committed to revolutionising education. They dreamt of a world where learning was at the forefront, unburdened by the complexities of digital tools. Yet, in their sprint to outpace competitors, I sensed something wrong. The urgency in feature prioritisation, the rush, something didn't quite add up. When the curtain lifted, it revealed the real motivator: contractual obligations with educational institutions. Payments would only flow once certain product modules were up and running.

Here's the thing: while business methodologies are crucial, what truly drives me is the end user's experience. How can I contribute to a product that transforms lives? But to achieve that, I need transparency. I need to fathom the depth of business intentions to integrate them into our product blueprint.

While books and theory offer us a guideline, a 'North Star,' if you will, real-world scenarios seldom play by the book. Navigating this requires understanding, flexibility, and a lot of empathy. It's about discerning the vision, even if it's not textbook perfect. It's about advocating for the product, the end-user, and the business's best interests.

As Product Professionals, our role is diverse. While vision and strategy may sound high-flown, they're essentially our tools. Tools we employ to bridge the gap between businesses and their users, ensuring a harmonious collaboration that benefits all. It's not just about knowing the steps; it's about feeling the music and guiding everyone to the dance floor.

CHAPTER THREE

Getting hands-on

In the business realm, where strategy is the thread and vision the pattern, a subtle yet profound element often gets overlooked: managing expectations. It might seem a straightforward task for the uninitiated, eager to tick off boxes on a checklist. Yet, for Product Professionals, it's a delicate dance between ambition and reality, desires and deliverables.

◆ ◆ ◆

Expectations Management

In digital strategies, product visions, and business objectives, expectations management is the quiet sentinel that guards the gates of contentment. It bridges between what a client envisions and what is pragmatically achievable. But why is this so important?

When presented with a task, there's a natural inclination to dive deep, to surpass and astound. The glamour of exceeding expectations is tempting. After all, isn't going above and beyond the mark of excellence?

Let's pause for a bit, because here lies the paradox. In the eagerness to impress, one might inadvertently go astray. This delicate balancing act is where the art of managing expectations comes to the fore.

Recall the startup committed to revolutionising education or the multinational aiming to integrate OKRs seamlessly into its fabric. There's a hidden subplot of expectations of what the product should achieve, how users should benefit, and when deliverables should materialise. As a Product Professional, navigating these often tumultuous waters requires skill, both in communication and in action.

Firstly, it's about setting clear boundaries. Open dialogue with clients or stakeholders at the outset can preemptively address any misalignment between aspiration and capability. This initial phase is not about curbing enthusiasm but about channelling it in the right direction. It ensures that the roadmap drawn is ambitious yet anchored in reality.

Secondly, adaptability plays a huge role. Changes are inevitable. Market dynamics shift, user preferences evolve, and technological advancements surge ahead. Thus, managing expectations isn't a one-time event but rather a continuous process. As new challenges emerge, recalibrating client expectations becomes extremely important.

Additionally, managing internal expectations is just as crucial. As Product Professionals, we often juggle multiple hats. While pushing the boundaries is commendable, it's essential to recognise limits. Understanding one's capabilities and ensuring that internal teams are aligned is fundamental. After all, a promise is only as good as its delivery.

Understanding a client's vision, aspirations, and even fears, lends invaluable insight. It's not just about managing what they expect in terms of deliverables but also addressing the underlying emotions and motivations.

Managing expectations, while seemingly a task like any other, is profoundly human at its core. It's about trust, understanding, and mutual respect. As we weave the narrative of product development, this element ensures that the story resonates, satisfies, and, most importantly, meets the aspirations of all involved. In the grand scheme, it's not just about meeting expectations but about crafting a journey where everyone feels valued and heard.

◆ ◆ ◆

Requirements Management

This is the foundation of successful projects. But what does it entail, and how can we navigate its terrain?

At its core, requirements management revolves around the art of information gathering. Like a detective piecing together clues, it involves collating pertinent details to craft a clear picture of the project's needs. This information lays the foundation upon which every subsequent project phase is built.

There's an entire arsenal of tools at your disposal for this endeavour. Document analysis can unravel nuances from existing information. Focus groups offer collective insights, drawing from diverse viewpoints. Individual interviews, on the other hand, dive deep into specific perspectives, unearthing granular details. Then there's brainstorming, where free-flowing ideas create a fountain of potential requirements. Workshops can collate these diverse perspectives, fine-tuning them into coherent demands. Reverse engineering can reveal latent requirements for those inheriting existing projects, while surveys provide a broad, demographic-based understanding.

But remember, this isn't about adopting *every* method. It's about tailoring a unique blend that's suitable for your context. A systematic yet adaptive approach is a must. Mix, match, and cook up the perfect requirements-gathering recipe unique to your project's flavour.

A significant principle to remember is clarity. Recall our discussion on design thinking. The same principle applies here as articulating problems was crucial in ensuring a deep understanding. It's not enough to simply gather requirements; they must be distilled into a lucid form that can be communicated effectively.

This clarity finds resonance in Agile practices too. Think of the refinement meetings where the product person elucidates the intricacies of each user story. It's all about efficient communication, where team members assimilate the business rationale, evaluate the magnitude of the effort and flag ambiguities. Then it's up to the Product professional to either provide immediate clarity or revisit the drawing board, refining requirements until they're clear for estimation. We'll cover this in more detail a bit later.

In essence, requirements management is more than just a step in the process; it's a continuous dialogue, a dynamic interchange of ideas and clarifications. The goal? To translate abstract needs into tangible action points, laying the groundwork for project success. So, venture into this endeavour with an open mind, a keen ear, and a clear voice, ensuring every requirement is gathered and thoroughly understood.

The Pulse of Effective Requirement Management

Business acumen isn't just a fancy term; it's the lifeblood of effective requirement management. Imagine being dropped into an alien landscape and expected to navigate without a map. That's what stepping into a business scenario without the appropriate level of understanding feels like. So, what exactly is "business acumen"? It's the hunger, the excitement to dive deep and grasp the nuances of a particular business or situation. But it's not just about surface knowledge. Actual business acumen means going even deeper, understanding the backdrop against which the company operates, its challenges, the opportunities it can capitalise on, and the risks it must navigate. In the Agile universe, a product professional with such profound insight isn't just an asset; they're a lighthouse guiding the entire project.

Speaking of risks, they're not just speed bumps on the road

to product completion. They're critical considerations that need to be spotlighted from the get-go. Potential risks should be on the radar from when a project is born. And as we traverse the journey from inception to conclusion, risks shouldn't just be spotted; they should be meticulously assessed and woven into the project planning. But it doesn't end there. Like vigilant sentinels, we need to oversee these identified risks throughout the project's execution, ensuring they don't morph into tangible threats.

When dissecting a risk, it's important to adopt a mixed approach. Identify the risk owner. Assess the risk's probability, asking: "What are the chances of this risk becoming a reality?" Next, measure its potential harm – the severity of its impact. Would it be a minor setback or a colossal catastrophe? And finally, and most importantly, brainstorm mitigation strategies. How can we preemptively defuse this risk or reduce its fallout? In summary, business acumen isn't just an attribute but rather a holistic perspective. It demands an understanding that extends beyond the immediate task, encompassing the broader business ecosystem.

Story Mapping

The journey of product development is one of constant refinement, and at the heart of this process lies story mapping, a powerful tool that gives shape and structure to your product vision.

Story mapping is charting user stories on two dimensions:

- Horizontal Axis: This signifies the user activities arranged based on their priority or the sequence you'd typically employ to explain the system's behaviour.
- Vertical Axis: Reflects the depth or sophistication level of the implementation. The higher you go, the more intricate the details.

Envision this map: the topmost row showcases a stripped-down yet functional version of your product. As you navigate through each successive row, functionalities and features are added.

The Genesis of the Map

The stories that populate this map aren't new. They trace back to the brainstorming phase, where ideas germinated and will later morph into user stories. However, before diving deep into detailed acceptance criteria, it's crucial to lay out this map because it offers clarity and might inspire the creation of new stories or the refinement of existing ones because it eliminates the redundant effort and allows the team to laser-focus on pertinent aspects at each phase and because once the map's finalised, its contents feed into the Product Backlog.

User Stories

When we step into the realm of requirements, it's not just about "what" needs to be done but also "how" these requirements are conveyed to the team. Let's dive into "User Stories".

Imagine you're translating a beautiful poem from one language to another. You're not just translating words but also emotions, imagery, and essence. Similarly, user stories communicate between business stakeholders and the technical team, turning commercial needs into actionable tasks.

There's no such thing as a universal template that makes it all perfect, and that applies across the board. And if you think you've achieved perfection in writing your user stories, you might be surprised when you'll switch teams or projects.

With each and every interaction, with each and every new feature, your approach will slightly change. And that's ok. You are the one who needs to adjust so that the story you write reaches the desired aspect in terms of clarity and granularity and appeals to everyone's level of understanding.

The same User Story that you're writing needs to speak the language of the development team, who are technically savvy, but it must also speak the language of the business owners, who may or may not have a technical background.

My definition of a perfect User Story has its foundation in the following idea: if you take a stranger from out on the street and show them the User Story you've written, they should understand it. It should be fairly easy for anyone to wrap their heads around the requirement, the context, and the functionality that will be born as a result of implementing that particular User Story.

What is a User Story?

A User Story clearly represents a requirement, illustrating the user's perspective and articulating how a particular functionality will deliver specific value to the customers.

It is written as a story, using a specific format, but in plain English and in such a language that any human can easily read and understand with no prior context or additional information.

How granular is, in fact, a User Story?

Well, you've got Project level, Feature level, Epic level, and then you've got User Stories. So they are basically the single most granular expression of a requirement. However, as granular as it may be, a User Story still needs to define a fully testable and deliverable piece of functionality, no matter how small.

Why do we use user stories?

We use them to translate business needs into user-focused functionalities. We use them to create a common understanding of what we want to build (so that we end up building the right thing) and how it will be built (so that we end up building it the right way). We use them to have a single source of truth and a more standardised way of structuring and communicating within the team, but also outside the team, with our internal or external stakeholders. And last but not least, we use them to set up expectations and create habits.

What are the benefits of better User Stories?

Faster delivery, higher customer satisfaction, better learning curve, quicker decision making, less waste.

So, build the right thing and build it the right way, or else questions will arise, and not the good kind. The bad kind that will soon translate into uncertainty, lack of confidence, questioning and push-back, all the nasty things that will badly damage your relationship with the development team. Not to mention the delays, the late hours on Friday nights at the end of the sprint, the multitude of bugs that will inevitably creep into the product that you're supposed to be nurturing, and last but not least, barely solving for the need and low to no customer satisfaction. And remember to *INVEST* in good User Stories because User Stories need to be:

- *Independent*, so that they can be worked on without any type of dependencies.
- *Negotiable* because a User Story is not a contract for a feature.
- *Valuable*, meaning that it must deliver value for the customers.
- *Estimable*, to a reasonable level of approximation.
- *Small*, sized such that it fits into an iteration.
- *Testable* so that the conditions of success can be tested.

The anatomy of a User Story.

You can have different types of User Stories: you can have regular User Stories, you can have Technical User Stories, or you can have SPIKEs, which are basically investigation User Stories.

What makes a good User Story?

To begin with, a User Story has a title. The title must be concise, clear, and intuitive. Think about newspaper headlines. That's what the title is to your User Story.

Then it's best to provide a bit of context as to why is it that we want to implement this piece of functionality, what value it brings to our customers, and what need it solves.

This is because the development team cannot work in

isolation. They don't just sit around in a bubble waiting for someone to feed them user stories without them understanding the full context and the implications.

The better they grasp the context of the requirement, the more capable they'll be of coming up with a better technical solution, and with valuable feedback for the business.

How do we express that context? Well, as part of the anatomy of a user story, you begin with the famous "As a / I want / So that" formula.

Let me give you an example: if the title of my user story is "A user can perform a search on the website", then the expression of the context would be:

As a website user
I want to perform a search on the website
So that I can find the item that I'm looking for

Then you've got the Acceptance Criteria section. This is where you write down the actual requirement. Because the context is not a requirement, it is a mere high-level description of the reasoning behind the requirement.

What you will write down in the Acceptance Criteria section, the development team will turn into reality. The developers will write the code, and the testers will test the functionality afterwards. And the Product Owner or the Business Analyst will perform the UAT (User Acceptance Testing) based on these specific requirements.

What should the Acceptance Criteria look like?

Ideally, you would structure it in Scenarios. For example, Scenario No 1, Scenario No 2, and so on. Each of them with a specific title and composition. And this is where we use the other famous body part of a User Story: the "Given / When / Then" sequence.

The **"Given"** is the prerequisite. It describes what you already need to have in place by the time you get to this step.

The **"When"** is the trigger. It shows what needs to happen in order to determine a specific behaviour.

"Then" is the expected behaviour. It illustrates what should happen as a result of a specific trigger.

Following our previous example, with the customer who needs to be able to perform a search on the website, our first scenario in the Acceptance Criteria would sound like this:

Scenario 1: the title will be: "Search option is available for the user"

Then we've got the "Given/When/Then" sequence:

Given that the user has accessed the website
When the "Products" page of the website is displayed
Then the "Search" module is available in the top-right corner of the screen.

What have we done here? First, we've described the prerequisite: "**given** that the user has already accessed the website". Why? Because if the user doesn't access the website, there's no functionality to speak of.

Then we specified the trigger: "**when** the Products page of the website is displayed". Why? Because the development team needs to know when this newly implemented piece of functionality should be available to the users. Do we want the "Search" functionality on all the pages of the website? No, we only want it to be available when you access the "Products" page. So the "When" is the trigger, remember that.

And only afterwards do we ask for the expected behaviour: "**then** the Search module is available in the top-right corner of the screen". That is because we need to illustrate what should happen if I accessed the website and landed on the "Products" page. The expected behaviour in our case is that now I can see a "Search" box.

So now we can see the search box on that page, but... how do we make it work?

Well, that's fairly easy: we write a second scenario as part of the Acceptance Criteria, with the following title: "The user can search for a specific product by name".

Following the "Given/When/Then" magic formula, here's what we've got:

Given that the user has submitted specific search criteria using the search input box

When the user clicks on the "Search" CTA (call to action)

Then the filtering is performed according to the specified criteria

And the search results list is displayed, containing all products matching the search criteria

One important note here: you can have multiple "Given" prerequisites or preconditions, and you can express them by using "and", for example: "**Given** that the user has submitted specific search criteria using the search input box, **AND** the search input box contains valid characters".

You can also have multiple "Then" expected behaviours, like, for instance, in our previous example: "**Then**, the filtering is performed according to the specified criteria. **And** the search results list is displayed, containing all products matching the search criteria".

But there can be only one "when". The trigger must be a singular expression, one single event.

Also, in terms of scenarios, we need to be careful to specify all possible cases: the happy case scenarios, the fail cases, and the edge case scenarios. And in order to do that properly, we need to walk a mile in our customers' shoes and always question every action and every decision. That's the only way we can maximise our chances of uncovering all possible use cases.

There you go, many things need to be considered when writing User Stories, and it's a process that should not be taken for granted.

Writing proper user stories, ones that the development team can easily understand and implement, ones that are clear, concise, and with the right amount and quality information, is an entire process that can either make your life easier or can cause nightmares and a lot of trouble.

Use all of this information as your North Star, even though most probably you won't be able to create a perfect User Story each and every time.

Product Backlog

The Role of the Product Backlog

Think of the Product Backlog as your compass, an exhaustive, ordered list capturing everything deemed essential for the product. It stands as the definitive guide for requirements.

Who champions this list? The Product person, mainly the BA or PO. They nurture the backlog, ensuring its contents remain up-to-date, accessible, and well-ordered.

We can distinguish between two distinct categories: the product backlog and the sprint backlog. Items that shine in clarity and boast high priority gracefully transition from the product to the sprint backlog, awaiting action.

Every item in the backlog has an intrinsic business value. This value often ties back to monetary gains post-release. However, it's essential to understand that not all worth is minted in gold. Sometimes, retaining a license or avoiding potential pitfalls carries weight.

Determining an item's business value is a challenging task. It leans on informed reasoning, cost-benefit analyses, market-entry timing, legal imperatives, and compliance mandates. However, decisions are inevitable.

A well-managed backlog operates in clear tiers:

- High Priority: These items have been fleshed out in detail, making them prime candidates for the sprint backlog.
- Low Priority: These lurk in the distant corners of the product backlog, characterised by their broad, high-level requirements.

Yet, there is always a guiding star: the customer. Their needs reign supreme, setting the stage for other factors like anticipated revenue, competitive pressures, partnership dynamics, or associated risks.

Backlog management centres around discerning and prioritising value. While numerous variables come into play, the customer's needs are the undeniable cornerstone. Only once we cater to them can we address the multitude of other considerations that feed into backlog prioritisation.

Backlog Refinement

With a populated and prioritised product backlog, the stage is set for refinement sessions. These interactive meetings see the Product person elucidating business requirements to the team. Here, queries are addressed, clarifications are sought, and, if necessary, tasks to gather more information are assigned. The culmination of these sessions? Estimates. The team assesses each user story's complexity, typically quantified in story points.

In sum, the refinement process is a symbiotic blend of mapping, prioritising, and estimating, each step building on the previous to ensure a product's successful realisation.

The Art and Science of Estimation

The act of estimation, in the realm of agile software development, is much more than just assigning numbers to tasks. It's a meticulous process that reflects the team's understanding and constantly evolves based on experience.

Setting the baseline

Establishing a baseline is crucial for a developing team. This involves choosing a user story, preferably of medium complexity, and using its estimation as a benchmark. Conventionally, such a story is pegged at three story points. This mid-range value offers flexibility, allowing for more straightforward tasks to be marked lower (at 1 or 2 points) and more intricate ones higher (at 5 or 8 points). A rule of thumb? Avoid stories valued at 13 points or more; these are often too vast to be tackled within a 2-week sprint.

The Evolving Nature of Estimations

Teams aren't static. As they evolve, so does their expertise. The story that once held a 3-point value might be perceived as a 1-pointer a few months later. It's a testament to their growing synergy and skill. This dynamic nature also underscores a critical principle: one team's estimates can never be juxtaposed against another's. They're unique, moulded by their collective experiences.

Planning Poker

One of the popular techniques employed for estimation is "planning poker". The essence? Members use numbered cards, representing their estimations, revealing them simultaneously. The advantage? It curtails the herd mentality, urging members to rely on individual assessments. Typically, these numbers trace the Fibonacci sequence: 1, 2, 3, 5, 8, and in rarer, complex scenarios, 13. Anything beyond that necessitates a breakdown into more digestible requirements.

Once the cards are on the table, the next step is deliberation. Differing estimates demand discussions, leading the team to unearth the rationale behind each number. Did someone's relative inexperience influence their estimate? Or perhaps there was a misunderstanding about the task's scope? These discussions foster consensus, nudging the team towards a shared understanding and estimation.

A pivotal aspect of estimation is the clarity of the user story. Ambiguous or unclear stories are a recipe for skewed estimations.

If questions linger, the story remains unestimated until clarity emerges. This safeguards against the volatility of undefined requirements, which could significantly sway the final estimate.

While estimates provide direction, they aren't the destination. Committing to a user story is just the start of the journey. The real task lies in navigating the implementation nuances, ensuring the story sees its realisation. Estimation is a blend of art grounded in the team's intuition and science, honed by experience and iterative feedback. It's a dance of numbers, judgment, and collective wisdom.

Establishing Clarity in Agile

Navigating the agile landscape necessitates setting clear expectations. It's a compass that directs a team's journey, ensuring everyone is on the same page. Two pivotal navigational markers in this terrain are the 'Definition of Ready' and the 'Definition of Done'.

Definition of Ready

Before embarking on the sprint journey, it's crucial to discern if a user story is indeed 'ready' to be tackled. This readiness is determined by a checklist – the 'Definition of Ready' – crafted collaboratively by the team. If a user story fails to tick off all the criteria on this list, it's understood that the story won't be part of the upcoming sprint.

This definition isn't universal. Like each agile team's unique rhythm, their 'Definition of Ready' might differ based on their collective experiences and tenure together.

AA typical "Definition of Ready" might look like this:
- Clear specifications.
- Absence of roadblocks or inter-story dependencies.
- No third-party dependencies.

- Estimations within a maximum of 13 story points.
- Readiness and availability of designs and translations (when relevant).

Definition of Done

Just as it's important to ascertain the onset of a task, establishing its completion is equally essential. The 'Definition of Done' is that clarifying checklist. It marks the successful completion of a user story.

An illustrative "Definition of Done" might include:
- Successful passage of all tests.
- Comprehensive code review.
- Updated documentation.
- Fulfilled acceptance criteria.
- UAT (Successful User Acceptance Testing).

User Acceptance Testing (UAT)

UAT is the guardian at the delivery gates. It's the phase where the product professional scrutinises the implemented feature, ensuring it aligns with the specified acceptance criteria. If UAT unveils discrepancies, the product person can withhold approval, sending the story back for revisions. Thus, ensuring that the acceptance criteria are robust from the outset is vital.

A Taste Of Scrum

Scrum is a framework, and at its heart lies the principle of agility and responsiveness, creating a space where product development is structured and adaptable. This duality allows for a harmonized approach to product management where progression is not linear but rather iterative, characterized by cycles known as Sprints.

These Sprints, typically two to four weeks, serve as concentrated time frames where specific goals are set and achieved, fostering a sense of continuous momentum towards the overarching project objectives. It is essential to recognize Scrum's emphasis on cross-functional collaboration and self-organization.

Unlike other Agile frameworks, Scrum facilitates a democratic environment where team members have the autonomy to decide how to achieve their Sprint goals, promoting accountability and innovation. The roles within the Scrum framework, including the Scrum Master and Product Owner, support the team, ensuring a facilitative environment for peak performance and steering product development in alignment with the stakeholders' expectations.

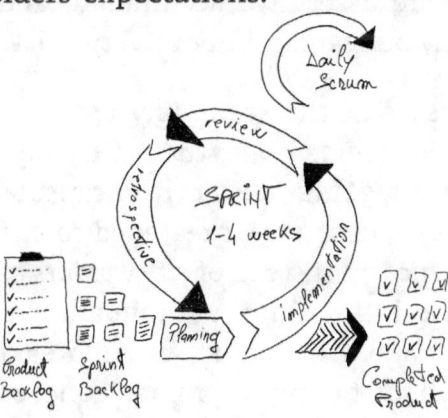

Through its iterative cycles, Scrum encourages a culture of frequent inspection and adaptation. This continuous feedback loop provides a more dynamic response to changing market conditions, technological advancements, and shifting project requirements. It essentially means that instead of a rigid progression through the development stages, teams have the latitude to revisit and refine aspects of the project, ensuring a product that is not only technically sound but also aligned with user expectations and market demands.

Adopting the Scrum framework can be a strategic move for organizations aiming to drive business success through products that meet market demands and create meaningful connections with their users.

◆ ◆ ◆

From the Trenches

Interestingly, in the realm of product management and business strategy, the skills we acquire don't just stay confined to our professional domain. They seamlessly transition into our personal lives. Every negotiation with a stakeholder, every exercise in active listening, every dive into the depths of a new business arena – these are not just tasks. They're life lessons in disguise. They're assets we accumulate and carry forward, enriching not only our careers but our very existence.

Take, for instance, the seemingly trivial act of estimating in unicorns. Been there, done that. On the surface, it may appear childish. But going deeper, it encapsulates the spirit of adaptability. When monotony threatened to stifle creativity, the introduction of *unicorns* instead of *story points* as a measurement unit breathed fresh life into a mundane task. The lesson? Innovation isn't always about groundbreaking revelations; sometimes, it's about taking a familiar concept and giving it a delightful twist.

Speaking about revelations, in my transition from banking to the field of product development, I was immediately struck by the refreshing new approach to collaboration and workflow. This excitement spurred a conversation with a close friend of mine who runs a construction company, where I began to explain the principles of Scrum that were guiding my new work environment.

As I detailed our morning meetings, or stand-ups, where we discuss progress and outline the day's objectives, as well as our regular planning sessions to reassess and prioritize tasks, I noticed a nod from my friend. He pointed out that these strategies were not as new as I thought; they were already a routine part of his operations on construction sites.

This interaction was a wake-up call, highlighting that beyond the buzzwords and industry-specific language, these strategies were essentially grounded in basic common sense. It underscored that the skills and insights I was acquiring were not confined to my field but were versatile and applicable to virtually any industry. It's all about organizing efficiently, maintaining open communication, negotiating effectively, and keeping a clear focus on your goals.

This conversation also reminded me that not all processes need to adhere strictly to a set guideline; rather, they can be adapted to better suit your unique needs and objectives.

Blending in, adjusting, and being adaptive are more than just survival skills in the professional wilderness. They are the hallmarks of growth, both personal and collective. But underlying all these traits is a fundamental principle: care. Genuine care. Care for your craft, for your teammates, for the end goal, and most importantly, for the journey itself.

CHAPTER FOUR

Collaboration and

stakeholder management

In this line of duty, understanding stakeholders is very important. But who exactly are these stakeholders? A stakeholder can be an individual, a collective, or an organisation either impacted by the project's results or having the ability to impact the project itself. Regardless of their origin, internal or external to the project's sponsoring organisation, stakeholders are invested in the project's success. Their influence, however, can swing positively or negatively.

◆ ◆ ◆

Stakeholder Categorization

Imagine a series of concentric circles, each representing different stakeholder categories:

- Innermost Circle - Sponsors: These are the project's backbone. They own the requirements and, ultimately, bear the responsibility for the project's success.
- Next Circle - Development Team: These are your problem solvers. They architect the technical solutions and ensure impeccable implementation.
- Third Circle - Reference Group: The auditors, in a way. They ensure the change doesn't ripple adversely. If there are ripples, they ensure alignment.
- Outermost Circle - Customers: The reason the project exists. These end-users reap the benefits of the entire product development process.

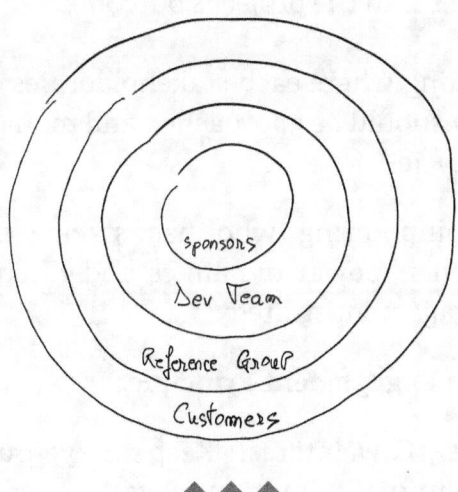

◆ ◆ ◆

Stakeholder Mapping

An effective technique involves plotting stakeholders on a two-axis table:

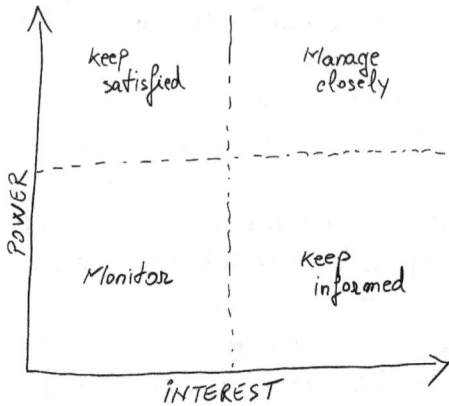

- Vertical Axis (Power): Represents the extent of a stakeholder's influence on the project.
- Horizontal Axis (Interest): Depicts how vested the stakeholder is in the project's outcome.

Understanding where each stakeholder lies on this grid can inform how they should be approached and managed throughout the project's lifecycle.

Begin by pinpointing who has stakes in your project. Understanding their power dynamics and interests is vital for determining engagement strategy.

Stakeholder Engagement Principles:

- Low Power, Low Interest: Keep an eye out, but they require minimal attention. Regular updates might suffice.
- High Interest, Low Power: They're keen on the project's progress, so ensure they're well-informed. Valuing their perspectives can be beneficial.
- Low Interest, High Power: Their influence is

significant despite their occasional detachment. Prioritise their needs and keep them content.
- High Interest, High Power: The top-tier stakeholders. Their interest and influence are at their highest peaks. Dedicate substantial effort to maintain a strong rapport and consistent engagement.

Engaging stakeholders isn't a one-size-fits-all game. It's imperative to truly understand stakeholders' perspectives and desires and to approach them tailored to their unique expectations and needs. Securing project outcomes isn't just about meeting goals but forging and nurturing relationships. By actively engaging and understanding stakeholders, relationships solidify, setting a positive precedent for future interactions while communication barriers diminish, streamlining the journey to success.

◆ ◆ ◆

Working Together In Cross-Functional Teams

Building a software product is all about teamwork. Everyone has a part to play in creating something that stands out and serves its purpose. The foundation of this is cross-functional teams. These teams, with their mix of skills and knowledge, are crucial for developing products that work and connect with users.

Think of software development as more than just coding. It's like a group project where each member brings different expertise —be it in engineering, design, marketing, user experience, or quality assurance. Unlike groups where similar experts cluster together, here, everyone brings a unique contribution. The goal? To make a product that combines technical strength, user-friendliness, and market readiness.

For someone managing the product, leading such a diverse team can be challenging. Everyone is an expert in their field and sees things from their unique perspective. Sometimes, what one team member proposes might seem challenging or time-consuming to another. The task is to balance innovation with practicality.

But when these different skills and viewpoints come together, the end product can be truly special. Different ideas lead to creative solutions. When problems come up, they're tackled from all sides, leading to well-rounded answers.

Of course, challenges exist. Sometimes, roles might overlap, or there can be too many opinions, leading to delays. Or, members might stick too closely to their individual roles, creating gaps in collaboration. It's up to the product leader to guide the team, ensure everyone has a clear role, and make decisions when needed.

Cross-functional teams are essential in software development. For those leading the product, they provide an opportunity to guide a diverse group towards creating something remarkable. With good communication, understanding, and leadership, the team can produce a product that's not just functional but truly outstanding.

The Dynamics Of Distributed Teams

Geographical boundaries have faded, replaced by the ticking of time zones that govern global work rhythms. Here, distributed software development teams have found their groove. While they present vast opportunities, they also come with their own unique challenges.

Distributed teams, often called remote teams, work towards a shared objective but from different locations, be it different cities or continents. The beauty of this model? Companies can tap into global talent and potentially cut costs by operating in regions with lower expenses. Plus, with team members in different time zones, work can, theoretically, go on around the clock.

Yet, the spread of these teams also poses problems. The distance can complicate communication. Varied time zones disrupt real-time discussions, while language and cultural differences can lead to misunderstandings. Collaboration can become slow, and fostering team spirit – often crucial to success – becomes challenging in a world dominated by screens.

Managing performance from afar requires fresh approaches. Yet, by using tech tools like Slack, Zoom and Jira, the challenges of distance can be minimised. In the remote world, the key is often to communicate more, not less: regular updates, check-ins, and feedback keep everyone aligned. Recognising and respecting cultural differences can enhance team cohesion. Celebrating global festivals or holding multicultural bonding events can build unity. Clear goals and timelines ensure everyone's on the same page. Offering flexible work hours can cater to personal routines. And while virtual meetings are the norm, occasional face-to-face gatherings can bolster team morale and relationships.

As we adapt to this model, it's vital to grasp its nuances.

Guided by empathy, creativity, and adaptability, distributed teams can indeed set new standards for global collaboration.

Cultural awareness

Product Professionals (PPs) often find themselves collaborating with teams that stretch across continents. Each member of these teams brings more than just professional expertise; they carry with them a wealth of cultural experiences and insights.

Clear communication is the foundation of any successful team, and nowhere is this more crucial than in distributed teams. In some cultures, for instance, direct disagreement is sidestepped in favour of politeness. A PP, aware of such nuances, will be adept at reading between the lines, ensuring that the team's communication remains effective and misunderstandings are minimised.

Trust, the foundation upon which collaborations are built, is cultivated differently across the world. In some places, trust may be established through consistent work deliverables, while in others, it's nurtured over extended periods through the establishment of personal relationships. Recognising and adapting to these varied approaches ensures a harmonious and effective working relationship.

Furthermore, embracing cultural awareness can enhance decision-making. By tapping into the collective intelligence and diverse perspectives of the team, decisions become richer, more nuanced, and more reflective of the global audience they serve.

Practical strategies can assist PPs in this journey. Celebrating diverse holidays, from Diwali to Hanukkah, can foster a sense of unity and inclusivity. Scheduling challenges due to varying time zones can be met with flexibility, ensuring everyone feels respected. Similarly, being mindful of language—avoiding jargon or colloquialisms that might not resonate universally—keeps communication channels clear. Encouraging team members to share about their local customs or day-to-day lives can weave a fabric of mutual understanding and respect.

In the end, for today's PPs, the task is not just to create a product that resonates globally but to do so while valuing and guiding a multitude of talents. It's about understanding that words can carry different weights in different cultures, that work habits can vary, and that trust is built in many beautiful ways. Embracing and celebrating the cultural diversity within teams elevates not just the products created but also the very essence of collaboration, fostering an environment where everyone feels valued and cherished.

Ideas, timelines, and deliverables constantly intertwine, yet feedback is guiding every move. For Product Professionals navigating cross-functional global teams, grasping the nuances of feedback isn't merely essential; it's transformative.

In product development, feedback is more than just a set of comments. It becomes an exercise in active listening, a journey into discerning underlying concerns and moulding them into actionable strategies. This task takes on new dimensions when one interacts with a team scattered across various locations. These variations, carved by unique cultural, professional, and personal experiences, offer a glimpse into the product's evolution.

Decisions grounded in varied feedback offer a comprehensive view, shaping a product that resonates on a global scale. Moreover, when team members witness their feedback influencing product trajectories, it instils a profound sense of belonging and boosts morale.

Harnessing feedback to its fullest potential requires a multifaceted approach. It's vital to employ a multitude of mechanisms, from surveys and focus groups to real-time tools seamlessly integrated into collaboration platforms. With the global backdrop, it becomes imperative to recognise and appreciate the cultural undertones of feedback. Some cultures might offer straightforward critiques, while others might convey them in subtler tones. Periodically, consolidating feedback helps in discerning patterns, identifying commonalities, or spotlighting recurring concerns. Furthermore, after feedback has been incorporated, it's crucial to circle back to the team, reinforcing the idea that their insights were instrumental in shaping outcomes.

However, this feedback journey isn't devoid of challenges. Global teams, with their diverse voices, invariably produce an overflow of feedback. Extracting actionable insights from this vast pool can be a difficult task. Also, feedback from non-native speakers might come layered with cultural and linguistic nuances, demanding a deeper level of understanding.

It's, therefore, beneficial to have systems that prioritise feedback based on its relevance, urgency, or overall importance. Regular feedback exchange sessions can ensure that voices from various corners of the globe find a resonant platform. Engaging individuals familiar with cultural nuances can be pivotal in ensuring the essence of feedback, especially when steeped in cultural context, remains intact.

Feedback operates as a beacon. By finetuning feedback mechanisms, the aim isn't merely product enhancement but an acknowledgement of the collective wisdom of a varied team. In striking this balance, both product success and team harmony find their rhythm.

◆ ◆ ◆

From the Trenches

In 2020, the world was blindsided by the Covid-19 pandemic, changing the way we live and work. It was a stark reminder that we're all in this together, regardless of where we come from. At that time, I was working for a large multinational company, already accustomed to the remote work model. Still, even I felt the weight of being forced into this setup without a choice.

However, as the months went by, the global community of professionals found ways to adapt. What stood out was our ability to connect on a deeper, more personal level. We learned to tackle challenges and cultural differences, building trust and fostering teamwork along the way.

One of the most memorable experiences during this period was when I accidentally joined a client's psychological group counselling session. I was met with open arms, understanding and kindness, and I seamlessly became part of the group. This moment highlighted that, in the face of a global crisis, our shared humanity shines through. Differences in job titles, cultures, and backgrounds become secondary.

Understanding this shared human experience isn't always straightforward. It's like peeling layers off an onion to get to the core of it. Being open and setting aside our biases helps in truly connecting with others. While there's a risk in being vulnerable, it often leads to genuine connections.

CHAPTER FIVE

Inner harmonies

In our shared human quest for happiness, an undeniable truth exists: happiness is not a permanent state but a fleeting emotional response to particular outcomes. It's as brief as a gust of wind or the shimmer of a dewdrop in the morning sun.

◆ ◆ ◆

The Labyrinth Of Personal Truths

So, what should be our guiding compass in this ever-shifting landscape of emotions and desires? As much as we might wish otherwise, life isn't a stage where applause and accolades measure success. Blindly chasing universal acclaim or perpetual euphoria can lead us astray from our core and into a maze where our true selves get lost.

The key to navigating this maze lies not in constantly expanding our horizons but in deliberate constriction. While it might seem paradoxical in our contemporary world, brimming with many choices, there's profound wisdom in limitation.

By reducing our options, we sift through the noise, focusing only on what aligns with our soul's deep stirrings. We need to ask ourselves: what is the return on investment for our expended energies and moments? Pinpointing this can empower us to tailor our futures, directing our efforts towards endeavours that offer profound personal satisfaction.

Yet, among the many metrics we employ to measure our life's decisions, one often remains overshadowed: the tranquillity of our spirit. An age-old proverb says that "An honest man's pillow is his peace of mind". This encapsulates the essence of authentic living. Each night, as we lay our heads down, the accurate measure of our day isn't in its achievements or failures but in the peace that emanates from choices that mirror our genuine selves.

And while the road ahead often appears blurred and uncertain, our past can light the way. The future may be a puzzle, its pieces scattered and unclear, but our history holds the template. As we can't forecast every twist and turn, looking backwards, and reflecting on bygone days, decisions, and their resultant paths, can offer a treasure trove of insights.

These reflections, infused with lessons and understanding, can illuminate our path forward, ensuring that each step and choice resonates with our authentic self.

◆ ◆ ◆

The Paradox Of Self-Preservation

At first glance, placing oneself at the forefront might seem self-centred. However, safeguarding our mental and physical well-being often prepares us to better cater to those around us. Consider this aeroplane analogy: in moments of crisis, our innate impulse may drive us to shield and support our dearest ones. However, we need to pay attention to our own safety in these efforts to ensure our ability to be of any help at all.

The aeroplane's dropped oxygen masks serve as a potent metaphor for life. Before turning to aid others, the directive to put on our own mask first isn't rooted in a doctrine of self-interest but in practical wisdom. By fortifying ourselves and ensuring our own stability, we can extend our hand far more effectively to those in need. This principle isn't limited to the confined quarters of an aircraft. It's a broader life lesson.

Prioritising self-care isn't a retreat from our obligations or an indicator of diminished empathy. On the contrary, it's about optimising ourselves—our energy, our resilience, our compassion —so that when we step forward to give, support, and nurture, we do so with our fullest capacity. Often, actions that may bear a facade of self-concern may, in fact, be profound acts of altruism in the deeper scheme of things.

Life isn't merely a series of passive responses to the caprices of fate. It's about deliberate decisions, introspective evaluations, and striving to remain anchored to our genuine selves—even when that means steering against the currents of societal conventions or anticipated judgments.

Ernest Hemingway said that "*The best way to find out if you can trust somebody is to trust them*". How about starting with ourselves?

◆ ◆ ◆

The Dance Of Moments And Choices

"Life is not promised tomorrow."

This feeling, deeply embedded in our collective consciousness, serves as a reminder of human fragility. Each breath, heartbeat, and fleeting thought emphasises our ephemerality in this vast universe.

But, beyond the morbid reality of this statement lies a more profound, more resonant truth: our lives are not quantified by mere existence, the ticking of clocks, or the turning of calendar pages. Instead, they are defined by moments - exhilarating, heart-wrenching, and everything in between - that take our breath away.

When we look back on our lives, we often remember those instances that made us feel the most. The first heartbreak, the overwhelming joy of achievement, the sting of failure, the warmth of a loved one's embrace. These are the moments that shape our narrative. And in each of these moments lies a choice. A choice to retreat or advance, change or remain the same.

The shared nature of human experience is obvious in our shared emotional reactions. While our paths diverge, branching into different journeys with unique stories to tell, the essence remains the same. Regardless of race, creed, or background, we all bleed the same shade of red. It's a symbolic representation of our shared human experience.

Our joys and sorrows, victories and defeats, may look different on the surface, but they are profoundly and inherently human at their core. And it is this shared humanity that bridges gaps, enabling empathy, understanding, and connection. However, in its infinite wisdom, life isn't a peaceful lake, but rather a raging ocean. It thrives on friction and on challenges that test our spirit. While often seen as an antagonist, this friction is the catalyst for growth. Every stumble and obstacle pushes us towards evolving, becoming versions of ourselves we never imagined.

It compels us to question, to introspect. "Do you have the guts to fail?" This isn't just a question; it's a challenge. A challenge that urges us to evaluate our perceptions of success, our fear of the unknown, and our willingness to step out of our comfort zones. Failure, contrary to popular belief, isn't the end. It's a detour, often leading us down paths we would have otherwise overlooked.

Venturing beyond the known, the lack of comfort is undeniably intimidating. It's like standing at the edge of a ridge, unsure of what lies below. But what's more haunting than the fear of the leap is the shadow of the "what ifs" - the ghosts of unexplored possibilities, dreams unchased and ideas unexplored. These are the ghosts that linger, reminding us of untapped potential.

We must do things we've never done to gain what we've never had. While the path may be packed with uncertainty, it's also paved with infinite possibilities. Because every choice, every moment, and every challenge is an invitation to dance with life, to mould our destiny one step at a time.

◆ ◆ ◆

The Lone Wolf And The Alpha

"There is no power for change greater than a community discovering what it cares about." Margaret J. Wheatley

Solitude. Communion. Two sides of the same coin, yet often perceived as contrasting paths. There's an intrinsic romance associated with the lone wolf, the self-reliant wanderer carving their path, succumbing to nothing other than their instincts. They symbolise raw determination, an individual's strength in facing the vast wilderness of life.

Contrastingly, the Alpha, as leader of the pack, is seen as the symbol of unity and strength in numbers. Theirs is the task of connecting disparate personalities, weaving them into a cohesive force, leading them towards a common goal. It's about manoeuvring group dynamics, fostering trust, and elevating the collective spirit.

But who truly is more heroic? Is it the one who treads the desolate terrains on their own or the one who, with camaraderie, ensures that no one is left behind? The profundity lies in the realisation that they are not mutually exclusive. Each is a facet of the same journey, a phase in our continuous evolution. We all have moments of solitude, of introspection, where our fears and ambitions are our only allies. In these moments, we grow, evolve, and discover our core.

Yet, a time also comes when our journey intersects with those of others. Here, we recognise the importance of community, mutual growth, and shared successes. At their heart, an Alpha is that lone wolf who has embraced the beauty of togetherness. They've scaled personal peaks and are now seeking to guide others through their journeys.

Understanding and embracing one's vulnerabilities and fears are at the heart of this balance. By confronting our internal adversaries, we prepare ourselves to face external challenges. Fear is not an enemy; it's a compass. It directs us towards areas needing growth where our trust might need to be stronger.

Building trust is like nurturing a plant. It requires patience, understanding, and above all, genuine care. It's a visceral bond, often intuitive, always transformative. And while it may not be taught, it can be felt and shared. To find belonging, one must first belong to oneself.

To feel at home in a crowd, one must first feel at home in solitude. This harmony, this dance between solitude and togetherness, propels us forward, reminding us that our journey is always one of discovery, growth, and profound understanding, whether alone or together.

In Trust We Thrive

"Truth is, everyone is going to hurt you. You've just got to find the ones worth suffering for." Bob Marley

Trust isn't just a mere feeling; it's the foundation upon which our personal and professional interactions are built. It transcends the basic notion of belief and encompasses elements like vulnerability and risk-taking. After all, to trust is to make yourself susceptible to potential harm or betrayal, all in the pursuit of building more robust, resilient relationships.

In the professional environment, trust is layered. At its core, trust remains fundamentally about keeping promises and acting with integrity. But within an organisational context, it grows more complex. Here, trust interweaves with alignment to a common purpose, a shared vision, and mutual objectives.

Imagine for a moment that you're part of a corporate team. You'd expect each member to have the skills needed for the task at hand and align with the company's mission. This is where professional trust deepens from essential reliability. It evolves to encompass faith in a colleague's alignment with shared goals, commitment to the common cause, and confidence in their motivations aligning with the organisation's values.

Consider the act of delegation as an example. In entrusting a task to a colleague, you do more than just believe they'll complete it. You're expressing faith in their judgment, ability to make decisions in line with the company's values, and commitment to deliver results that benefit the wider group.

Furthermore, in the professional realm, competence takes centre stage. It's not just about integrity but also the assurance that someone can deliver on their promises. In a business setting, trustworthiness isn't just moral. It's also about skill, expertise, and the ability to execute.

In essence, while trust remains rooted in the basics of integrity, reliability, and sincerity, it blossoms into something more expansive in the corporate world. It becomes a mixture of shared purpose, aligned motivations, and proven competence. It's about navigating the maze of professional dynamics with both heart and skill, ensuring that you are reliable in action and sincere in intent at every turn.

The Anatomy Of Self-Belief

"Doubt kills more dreams than failure ever will." Karim Seddiki

"Believe in yourself!" It's an anthem we often hear. The ever-echoing chorus in the background, urging us on, willing us to take the next step. Yet, what does it genuinely confine? To believe in oneself isn't a blanket term, an all-encompassing affirmation that suddenly clears all our doubts. Instead, it's a spectrum, a mosaic of self-awareness, self-acceptance, and self-improvement.

Firstly, a fundamental truth - no one is universally proficient. We all have strengths and weaknesses. Recognising them doesn't detract from our self-belief; it amplifies it. In acknowledging our limitations, we also identify our capacities. As Matthew McConaughey aptly points out, there's a marked difference between "thinking you're a champion and knowing you are". The former might be a delusion, the latter a realisation of one's true potential in a particular sphere.

That said, self-awareness is the cornerstone of genuine self-belief. It's the ability to evaluate oneself objectively, celebrate one's strengths, and work on one's areas of improvement. And herein lies a crucial distinction.

While we must be wary of overestimating our abilities, we must equally guard against selling ourselves short. The journey to building self-belief isn't just about understanding where we shine and amplifying areas where we might only glimmer for now. Pursue knowledge, seek mentorship, and embrace experiences. Every effort made in the direction of improvement bolsters our self-assurance.

To indeed "have faith in oneself" is not about unwavering confidence in every aspect of our being. Instead, it's about nurturing a growth mindset, appreciating our intrinsic worth, and relentlessly pursuing evolution. It's the understanding that while we might not be perfect, we are perpetually perfecting.

So, the next time someone says, "Believe in yourself!" take a moment. Reflect upon where you've been, where you are, and where you're headed. Remember, it's not about groundless confidence. It's about fostering a solid foundation for that belief, brick by brick, experience by experience. Only when we genuinely know our worth can we confidently chart our path forward, fortified by the strength of our self-belief.

From the Trenches

I still remember it like it was yesterday, the first time I took an interview. The office setting, the freshly printed questions, the indistinguishable blend of excitement and anxiety in the air. But what I remember most was Laura, a young candidate with dreams in her eyes and a palpable drive.

Despite the novelty of the situation, I had this strong feeling that the series of generic questions I had been given was not the path to discovering her. I could have continued down the rehearsed path, checking boxes off the list. But by the time the third question rolled around, my instincts screamed for a change. I discarded the script, and instead of an interviewer, I became a genuine partner in conversation. Instead of a candidate, Laura became a storyteller.

This approach was to shape my interview style. Over the years, I've talked to hundreds of hopeful people, venturing beyond the bounds of their CVs and exploring their aspirations, passions, and fears. In its truest sense, interviewing became a part of my missions to understand the essence of other people.

But this journey hasn't been without its challenges. People, driven by past experiences or self-doubt, often come with protective barriers. To see their true potential, one must first navigate these emotional fortresses. Yet, the reward, when they open up, revealing the depth of their experiences and the breadth of their aspirations, is genuinely worth the effort.

Because everyone, without exception, has something valuable to offer. In Product Management, some skills are crucial, but they sometimes come in a different form than you'd expect. I've learned that a musician can understand rhythm and flow in a very nuanced manner, which is extremely valuable for assessing product usability. I've learned that a chemist offers analytical prowess, essential for data-driven decisions. How about a translator? They're experts in understanding and conveying nuanced messages, a vital skill for stakeholder communication. These are just a handful of real-life examples of people I've crossed paths with, and I've got many more just like these.

It's about spotting transferable skills, recognising what can be taught, and valuing what has been hard-earned through years of experience. It's about choosing your battles wisely, distinguishing between what's essential now and what can be cultivated over time.

But, beyond skills, experience, or even educational qualifications, one attribute stands out, one aspect that's the ultimate differentiator: desire. That burning passion, that unyielding drive, that insatiable thirst to learn and grow. This very fire can propel someone to greatness far more than any degree or accolade can.

Asking yourself what you truly desire is not just reflective but transformative. Knowing your innermost drive, acknowledging it, and staying true to it can help you surmount the highest obstacles. This drive, this passion, is something other than what any mentor or teacher can instil. It's intrinsic, born from within.

So, to every aspirant out there, whether at the cusp of your career or seeking a transformative shift, the real question isn't just about the skills you possess or the experience you've gathered. It's about the fire within you. So, once again, what is it that you truly desire? Find that answer, embrace it, nurture it, and let it lead the way. For with unwavering passion, there is no goal too distant, no dream too big!

CHAPTER SIX

Becoming the storyteller

"Stories have to be told, or they die, and when they die, we can't remember who we are or why we're here." - Sue Monk Kidd.

The timeless "Epic of Gilgamesh", carved onto ancient Babylonian tablets 4,000 years ago, continues to echo in the annals of literature. Yet, the tale's existence is not only a testament to its content but also its passage.

Over millennia, countless storytellers relayed the exploits of Gilgamesh, allowing the story to endure, crossing from one era to the next.

By contrast, consider the ancient cave paintings, humanity's earliest storytelling canvas. A recent discovery in Indonesia unveiled a depiction believed to be around 45,500 years old, marking it as the earliest known visual narrative.

But while these paintings catch headlines as significant archaeological findings, they seldom are revered as stories. Why is that?

At its core, while the cave painting might communicate an

idea or share a moment in time, it does not resonate with our emotions. Faced with the choice between an image of a pig and a hero's saga, which would capture your imagination and be worthy of your children's bedtime story?

Imagine if that singular cave painting was part of a series, each image building upon the other, weaving a tapestry of tales. Even so, a mural on a cave's wall can't sing its song or recite its verses. Stories need voices, and they need interpreters. A cave's solidity may preserve an image, but a Babylonian tablet's mobility can spread a narrative, lending credibility and sparking curiosity in distant lands and sceptical minds.

So always appreciate the power of storytelling. The content is vital, but the delivery, how you share, communicate, and resonate, that's what makes a tale immortal.

The Power Of Non-Verbal Communication

Professor Albert Mehrabian from the University of California, Los Angeles, defined in the 1970s the "7-38-55 Rule of Communication". Mehrabian's extensive research illustrated that words, while central to conveying a message, are only a subset of the primary communicators.

When breaking down the effectiveness of communication, he concluded that the words we use contribute a mere 7%. The tone of voice, the musicality and the cadence behind those words weigh in at 38%. The heavy lifter, surprisingly, is our body language, shouldering a whopping 55% of the message.

Revisiting the ancient piglet portrayal, it's clear that our Upper Paleolithic ancestors mastered the art of imprinting an enduring visual memory. Yet, the static image lacks a layered narrative's dynamic depth and richness. It remains an artefact devoid of the dynamism required to captivate and last through the ages.

Getting back to the legend of Gilgamesh, now that's a tale that beckons to be voiced aloud. Beyond its structured plot and impactful emotions, the story invites the orator to breathe life into it with a passionate tone and evocative gestures.

Drawing on Mehrabian's insights, a skilled storyteller can transport listeners to a bygone era, making it feel as though the mighty Gilgamesh himself stands before them, recounting his epic journey.

Effective communication transcends mere words. It's an immersive experience where voice and body work harmoniously to engrave a message into the soul of the audience.

"Storytelling is the greatest technology humans have ever created." - Jon Westenberg.

Why do humans, from our earliest ancestors to modern-day digital tenants, gravitate towards stories? Our natural quest for patterns is at the heart of our affinity for narratives. Our evolution as a species is intertwined with our exceptional ability to process patterns. Patterns provide clarity within chaos, a roadmap where none exists. They go beyond survival, hinting at our more profound desire to comprehend, connect, and eventually transcend.

Emotions act as the adhesive that binds these patterns, reinforcing their resonance. Thus, the power of a story emanates from the heart of the believer. A narrative shared with genuine emotion, which genuinely stirs the soul, is more likely to leave an indelible mark on its audience.

In today's digitalised age, we are all chroniclers. The digital universe swarms with tales, countless narratives awaiting discovery. Technology has democratised storytelling, allowing us to discern patterns, shape, stack, and share them. Out of this vast structural maze emerges raw, unbridled creativity.

Yet, the abundance of stories presents a dilemma: Which ones to embrace and champion? The compass guiding this choice lies within each of us. It's about resonance, about finding the narrative that strikes a chord with our innermost frequencies.

When a story truly moves the storyteller, it possesses the power to swing the world. The challenge is simple: if a tale fails to stir your spirit, it's unlikely to inspire others.

◆ ◆ ◆

Storytelling Across Eras And Platforms

Walt Disney said that *"In learning the art of storytelling by animation, I have discovered that language has an anatomy"*. This statement sheds light on the intricate weave of narrative across diverse mediums.

Storytelling, as an art, transcends the conventional. It spans from written epics to casual conversations, from profound books to contemporary apps. Even gossip, a seemingly frivolous act, is an informal narrative medium. It offers a mirror to social realities and fosters candid communication, facilitating instant feedback and perspectives for alignment.

A narrative's impact hinges on its resonance

Take the Bible, for instance. It boasts a staggering "user base" of about 5 billion. In contrast, Facebook, a modern behemoth, claims approximately 2.8 billion users.

While the Bible's inception remains enigmatic, oral traditions suggest its tales resonated across millennia, even before its official 1611 print by King James. Meanwhile, Facebook, a creation of 2004, skyrocketed in popularity within just a couple of years. Such rapid ascendancy indicates the tech giant might possess unique engagement tactics, potentially offering traditional religious institutions insights into fostering closer human connections.

Even though comparing the Bible and Facebook might strike some as inappropriate, while the Bible reverberates with timeless tales, often repeated to familiar audiences, Facebook chronicles diverse individual sagas, a vast tableau of human experiences. On Facebook, users select stories, react, and engage. However, while exploring biblical tales like "The Creation" or "The Universal

Flood", one's expressive scope remains limited. Although metaphors are enlightening, the restrictions on articulation in specific narrative spaces might feel stifling for some.

While vastly different, the Bible and Facebook share a core intent: fostering connection and rallying communities. As societies evolve, so should their narratives, adapting to resonate with shifting sensibilities.

This adaptability mirrors the challenges in product development. People don't merely invest in products or services; they buy into stories that touch their innermost needs and desires. In product development, marching forward isn't about blind obedience.

It's about understanding the why and the purpose. It requires empathising with customers and feeling their struggles. Only with genuine motivation can we support a cause and champion it fervently.

However, a story remains dormant without a narrator. It demands dedication: written with heart, spoken with enthusiasm, and shared with authenticity. Passion will reflect in the narrator's gaze, emotions in their tone, and faith in their every gesture.

Embrace storytelling, and you won't just employ but deeply experience humanity's most remarkable invention — storytelling.

The Hero's Journey In Product Development

Product development mirrors the art of storytelling in striking ways. Just as narratives weave tales that resonate and forge connections, the journey of creating a product is a collage of stories, from its nascent conceptualisation to the invaluable feedback from its users.

Storytelling in product management isn't merely about crafting an engaging narrative; it's about cultivating empathy, generating involvement, and guiding stakeholders along a transformative journey. This odyssey parallels the archetypal 'hero's journey' that transfuses countless tales across ages and cultures.

The 12 Stages of The Hero's Journey, conceptualised by Christopher Vogler and drawing inspiration from Joseph Campbell's "The Hero With A Thousand Faces", serves as a narrative blueprint for countless successful books and films.

This universal structure charts a hero's voyage: starting from their familiar surroundings, they journey into the unknown, face formidable challenges, and eventually return, having undergone a profound metamorphosis.

This cyclical narrative arc bears a remarkable resemblance to the product development lifecycle. Each iteration in product development is similar to a hero embarking on a new voyage, striving for excellence, and returning with insights that enrich the product and, by extension, the world.

So, as we embark on this exploration, let's dive deep into the product professional's hero's journey, unveiling the stages where myths and modernity intertwine.

Mapping the Hero's Journey to Product Management

The Ordinary World: Establishing Status Quo. As you step into the role of a product professional, you're introduced to the world as it currently exists. Whether your product is a newborn idea or a tangible tool serving real customers, you're in a phase of understanding, exploration, and gathering insights. It's your initial grounding, where you familiarise yourself with the landscape and comprehend the various facets of your product domain.

The Call to Adventure: Discovery Unleashed. As days pass, an unexpected challenge shakes your newfound peace. While you might have been anticipating disruptions, confronting them head-on, especially when they threaten customer satisfaction, can be unsettling. It rushes you out of your comfort cocoon, urging immediate attention and action.

Refusal of the Call: Deep Dives and Definition. While the urge to tackle the challenge is intense, pausing and dissecting the issue is crucial. In this stage, you delve deeper, researching, diverging, and converging to grasp the true essence of the challenge. It's also a time for introspection, where personal barriers might surface, compelling you to navigate and overcome them.

Meeting the Mentor: Ideation and Collaboration. A product professional's role isn't solitary. It thrives on collaboration and guidance. As challenges arise, seeking counsel, seeking feedback, and brainstorming solutions become invaluable. Surrounding yourself with knowledgeable allies, you entertain various ideas, refining them and bounding closer to your mission.

Crossing the Threshold: From Theory to Prototype. Armed with insights and ideas, you embark on a transformative journey. Moving beyond the familiar, you bring your hypotheses to life, crafting prototypes that embody potential solutions. This transition signals commitment, embracing varied dimensions, from the tangible to the intangible, as you venture forth.

Tests, Allies, Enemies: The Rigorous Test Phase. Plunging deeper into the unknown, challenges burst. Your prototype, your tangible representation of a solution, undergoes rigorous scrutiny. This phase is crowded with feedback, where judgement is critical. Identifying what aids your mission versus what hinders it is vital. Each hurdle crossed not only confirms the viability of your prototype but also furnishes a more profound understanding. Based on this, you must decide: Does your prototype require rework, or is it the blueprint for a lasting solution?

Approach to the Inmost Cave: Re-evaluating Foundations. Having encountered unexpected roadblocks during testing, you question both the solution and the initially identified need. This realisation calls for a retreat, a return to the foundational stages. With heightened intuition and empathy, your mission is to unearth the core necessity that demands resolution.

The Ordeal: Ensuring the Right Implementation. After a thorough revisit, you have a redefined problem and a validated prototype. Your next monumental task? Ensuring its impeccable realisation. Your audience changes at this juncture. As the customer's champion, you masterfully weave the narrative, translating it for various stakeholders. Between doubt and resistance, you stand committed to your vision and ready to tackle unforeseen challenges.

Reward (Seizing the Sword): Embracing Evolution Post Beta Release. The journey so far has been transformative. As you navigated hitches and bridged crests, you've grown as a product professional and an individual. While the prototype is a testament to your achievement, your evolution during the process is your most important reward. However, this victory is merely one phase, with many more battles awaiting.

The Road Back: Gearing up for feedback. Your creation now exists in the real world. While you've previously spoken on behalf of your users, it's now time to be all ears. Relinquishing personal biases and embracing early failures is extremely important, for they pave the path for swift recoveries. Treat your early users as allies, valuing their voluntary feedback and upholding their trust.

Resurrection: The GA Release Culmination. This moment signifies culmination and reckoning. As you unveil your product, the world awaits. Success is attributed to your team, but any lapse falls squarely on you. But with battles behind you, you face this moment with courage and conviction. This climactic phase determines your trajectory and repercussions for the larger environment.

Return With The Elixir: Post-GA Feedback Insights. As the journey completes, you return to familiar terrains as a renewed entity. The culmination is marked by enhanced knowledge, exposure to grave challenges, and profound transformations. The final insights, literal or symbolic, highlight change, accomplishment, and the journey's authenticity. As the tale winds up, sceptics face alienation, adversaries confront consequences, and allies bask in accolades. Though you're back where you started, the narrative, the world, and you have irrevocably transformed.

This analogy bridges the captivating world of hero tales with the intricate dance of product development. Each step, whether in an epic or the product lifecycle, is about growth, transformation, and the relentless pursuit of excellence.

CHAPTER SEVEN

Transitioning into Product roles

We often hear that only people with tech or business backgrounds can succeed in certain roles. However, as innovation grows, it's clear that this mindset is not only limiting but also counterproductive. In product roles, the varied experiences people bring can be a significant strength.

◆ ◆ ◆

Background Diversity And Transferable Skills

Background diversity becomes a critical aspect, not just a bonus. In the world of product management, terms like "MVP", "user stories", and "backlog prioritisation" might seem intimidating. You might think these are strictly for those well-versed in Product terminology. But the heart of product development is about understanding people, telling relatable stories, and solving tangible problems. It's here that different experiences really come into their own.

Take artists, for example. Their expertise in communicating emotions can offer deep insights into the user experience. They understand what people feel, can craft narratives, and visualise abstract ideas. This makes them great at designing user experiences that are more than just practical; they're also engaging.

Then there are those from a finance background. Their analytical skills and knack for understanding data can help guide a product's direction. While they might not be coding or designing, they play a crucial role in deciding if a feature is economically viable or predicting the impact of product changes.

Let's not forget about professionals in sociology or psychology, either. These fields dive deep into human behaviour. Their insights can be invaluable in designing products that not only work but also resonate with users on an emotional level.

The real benefits are seen when these diverse skill sets come together. Think about a brainstorming session where an engineer's logical mindset collaborates with an artist's creativity, a financial analyst's practicality, and a sociologist's understanding of human behaviour. The result is a comprehensive and user-focused product strategy.

As products cater to global audiences, it's also essential for the team to understand different cultures, preferences, and local needs. A diverse team can bridge the gap, ensuring a product appeals widely and not just in one region.

However, it's not about seeking diversity just for the sake of it. The key is to value and incorporate these varied viewpoints. Everyone, be it a former teacher, chef, or journalist, should feel just as valued in a product meeting as someone with a technical degree.

As our understanding of products evolves, we should continue to value and promote background diversity. The future of product roles isn't strictly about tech; it's also about the wide range of experiences and viewpoints people bring. The more we welcome this diversity, the better our innovations will be.

The Odyssey Of The Mindset

Every career move, like switching into product roles, requires more than just the right skills. It demands the right attitude. Changing careers isn't just about what you know but also how you think. Transitioning from a different field to roles like Business Analyst, Product Owner, or Product Manager requires adjusting your mindset in several significant ways.

Old habits can be hard to break. If you've spent years in a profession with unique practices and beliefs, diving into the fast-paced and often unpredictable world of product development can be challenging. It's like trying to adapt to a new environment: you need flexibility and a willingness to change how you approach problems.

One of the most significant shifts is going from relying on what "I think" to prioritising what "the user feels". In many jobs, decisions are top-down, based on what's always been done or what the higher-ups want. But in product roles, it's all about the user. Their feedback, needs, and preferences directly influence decisions. This requires setting aside personal biases and really listening to what users have to say.

◆ ◆ ◆

Another big change is embracing ongoing improvement. In many jobs, once a project is done, it's done. But in product roles, things are always evolving. Features are tested, changed, or even removed based on new data or feedback. This means being open to change and always looking for ways to improve.

Then there's the way you view risks. In some jobs, risks are something to be wary of. But in product roles, they're opportunities to try something new and make a real impact. It's about being willing to take chances, try new things, and learn from mistakes. It's not about being reckless, but about being open to exploring new possibilities.

Being open to collaboration is also essential. Product roles are all about teamwork. You'll work with designers, engineers, marketers, and others. If you're used to sticking to your lane, you'll need to get comfortable sharing ideas and blending your expertise with others.

We must also keep in mind the importance of continuous learning. The world of product development is always changing. New technologies and strategies emerge regularly. This means being eager to learn, willing to change your mind, and staying curious.

While having the right skills is crucial, it's the shift in mindset that truly makes the difference. Adapting to the unique challenges of product roles requires an inner journey. It's about becoming more flexible, open, and innovative. Remember, it's those who can adapt who succeed, especially in this world. This adaptability, and the mindset changes that come with it, are what will guide you towards success.

The Quest For Technical Acumen

During the Renaissance, figures like Leonardo da Vinci were admired for their expertise in various fields, from art to science. Today, with the rise of the digital era, there's a similar appreciation for versatility, especially in product roles. One key skill that's highly valued is a solid understanding of technology.

For those moving into roles like Business Analyst, Product Owner, or Product Manager from non-technical fields, the tech industry might seem overwhelming at first. Terms like APIs, frontend, backend, and cloud computing can be daunting. But behind these terms is a world of opportunity. Gaining a good grasp of technical concepts positions you at the heart of modern innovation.

This isn't about mastering coding but about understanding what technology makes possible. A Product Manager with technical insight can conceptualise product enhancements that are technologically viable. They're better equipped to judge the feasibility of an idea, foresee potential hurdles, and work closely with engineering teams.

Having a good technical foundation also improves communication. In product development, clear communication is crucial to avoid expensive mistakes. A technically-inclined Product professional can take user needs and turn them into clear directives, ensuring that a product's vision matches its final form.

Moreover, as technology advances, user expectations grow. People today want fast, intuitive, and smooth digital experiences. To meet these expectations, it's essential to keep up with new technologies, not just to understand their functions but to recognize their potential. Whether it's using artificial intelligence for custom user experiences or implementing blockchain for better security, a solid tech foundation places product professionals at the cutting edge of innovation.

So, how do you develop this skill? Start with a sense of curiosity. Talk to engineers to understand their mindset and approach. Keep up with tech trends by attending webinars and conferences. And most of all, be hands-on. Participate in prototype testing, dive deep into product design, and get to know the tools that bring digital concepts to life.

As we move further into the digital age, understanding technology is becoming essential. It's the tool that turns ideas into tangible products. For those entering product roles, this technical understanding is often the key to groundbreaking innovations.

Networking And Mentorship

Throughout history, many successful individuals, from explorers discovering new lands to scientists studying the universe, had someone or something guiding them. In product development, this guidance often comes from networking and mentorship.

Entering the world of product roles can be overwhelming, with a variety of challenges: understanding user needs, grasping market dynamics, and mastering technical details. But one key way to navigate these challenges is by building strong professional relationships.

Networking is more than just exchanging business cards or adding people on professional platforms. It's about building genuine connections with those who have similar goals and experiences. Whether you're having a casual conversation with a colleague or attending an industry seminar, each interaction provides insights and opportunities. Networking helps you understand the bigger picture of the industry, from emerging trends to best practices and common mistakes.

On the other hand, mentorship offers a deeper, more personal connection. With their extensive experience, a mentor helps you navigate potential challenges and guides you towards your goals. They offer advice on both the technical aspects of your job and the interpersonal dynamics of your workplace. A mentor helps you understand organisational nuances, improve your leadership skills, and build influential relationships.

The relationship between a mentor and a mentee is built on trust. It's a partnership where open discussions lead to a clearer understanding, and feedback is crucial for growth. A mentor is there to celebrate successes and provide support during tough times.

Having a mentor provides stability. They've faced similar challenges before and can offer guidance on adapting and staying resilient in the face of uncertainty.

As time passes, many mentees eventually become mentors, passing on their knowledge to the next generation. This continuous cycle of mentorship helps the industry grow, with each generation benefiting from the experience of those before them.

Traversing The Educational Pathways

Education is a crucial factor that ties our diverse experiences together. This is especially true in product development, where ongoing learning is essential. As individuals progress in roles like Business Analyst, Product Owner, or Product Manager, their educational journey plays a significant role.

For many, the journey starts with formal education. Degrees in fields such as business, technology, design, or even liberal arts lay the foundation for a career in product development. Each field offers a different viewpoint, whether it's the technical insights from an engineering degree, the user focus of design, or the broad thinking skills of liberal arts.

However, basic knowledge isn't always enough. That's where specialised training comes in, with courses, certifications, and workshops designed to dive deep into product-specific topics. These detailed studies transform beginners into professionals ready to tackle the various challenges of product development.

The digital age has also provided a wealth of self-paced learning options. Online platforms offer a range of courses and tutorials, allowing learners to move at their own speed. Here, individuals can focus on specialised areas, from data analytics to understanding user behaviour, creating a learning path that fits their career goals.

But learning isn't limited to the classroom. Real-world experiences, such as internships and hands-on training, provide invaluable lessons. Here, theoretical knowledge is put to the test and refined through practical application.

As product development becomes more interdisciplinary, the importance of diverse learning grows. A technical Product

Manager might benefit from courses on consumer behaviour, while a Business Analyst with a commerce background might delve into tech trends. Combining different educational backgrounds can lead to well-rounded professionals who can innovate and bridge knowledge gaps.

A career in product roles is a continuous educational journey filled with numerous opportunities to learn and grow. Formal education sets the stage, but it's complemented by specialised training, self-driven learning, and real-world experience. And it is not just about a one-time achievement; it's a lifelong process.

Challenges Of Transition

As someone embarks on roles such as Business Analyst, Product Owner, or Product Manager, they encounter a mix of excitement for new opportunities and apprehension about potential obstacles.

A common concern for many is the imposter syndrome. It's that nagging feeling where you doubt your achievements and worry that others will realise you're not "good enough." Questions like, "Am I qualified?", "Can I compare to my colleagues?" or "Will they find out I'm not what they expected?" can be overwhelming. However, realising this feeling is common among seasoned professionals can provide some relief. It's not a personal failing; it's a shared human experience.

But there's more to transitioning than just battling internal doubts. Each new role presents its own culture, terminology, team dynamics, and expectations. It might feel like you're navigating unfamiliar territory, even if you've been in similar roles before.

The key to adjusting is a combination of humility and assertiveness. It's okay to acknowledge what you don't know, but it's equally important to proactively seek out answers. Ask questions, clarify doubts, and invest time in understanding the new setting. Everyone, even experts, had to start somewhere and face the uncertainties that come with a new role.

Building connections is invaluable during these times of change. Interacting with colleagues, managers, and team members offers insights into the role and creates a network of support. Sharing your challenges, seeking feedback, and collaborating makes the transition smoother.

Additionally, celebrating small wins along the way can boost morale. Every task completed, successful meeting, or minor milestone reached confirms that you're on the right path and helps build confidence.

It's essential to remember that transitions are, by definition, temporary phases of adjustment. They're marked by ups and downs. Rather than aiming for immediate perfection, focus on steady growth and learning. Successes are built gradually, much like a beautiful piece of art that takes time and effort.

Moving into a product role or any new professional setting is a challenging yet rewarding journey. While internal doubts and the unfamiliarities of a new role can seem intimidating, these challenges become growth opportunities with the right attitude, resources, and support. Every hurdle overcome enriches the overall experience. After all, the journey and lessons learned along the way truly define our professional stories.

◆ ◆ ◆

From the Trenches

Throughout our careers, every experience and choice crafts a unique narrative. My journey took an unexpected turn when the subtle allure of teaching emerged beneath the layers of Product expertise. Five years into the vibrant world of product management, I transitioned from a novice to a mentor. This wasn't just about transferring skills; it was about igniting a passion, nurturing it, and watching it inspire others.

This mentoring spirit evolved into a structured training module, demystifying product management. Then, a serendipitous moment placed me in front of university students, equipped with my curriculum and met with their boundless enthusiasm. Their eagerness and curiosity became my driving force.

My passion led me to start my own company, offering tailored workshops across various organisational needs and introducing outsiders to the magic of product management.

From guiding countless individuals, I understood that product management is a welcoming field where anyone, regardless of their past, can thrive with dedication and persistence. However, a caveat: mastering this domain requires continuous effort and resilience. It's a challenging and intricate field, but therein lies its allure. Every day becomes an enriching expedition, contributing to one's growth.

My grandfather's wisdom resonates deeply with me: "Dive into endeavours with your whole being, as half-hearted attempts produce half-hearted outcomes." True success and fulfilment stem from pouring oneself completely into their pursuits. This isn't mere cinematic romanticism; it's a tangible reality achieved through genuine commitment, unwavering faith, and resilience during challenging times.

In summary, life's path isn't always straightforward. Yet, with unwavering passion and sheer determination, any storm can be weathered and any challenges surmounted. Success hinges on heartfelt dedication and taking bold, decisive actions.

CHAPTER EIGHT

Final thoughts

Innovation is often heralded as the ultimate business solution. However, transformative innovation – the kind that reshapes industries – isn't solely about novel products or services. It starts with an internal metamorphosis. True change in the external world begins with a personal journey of innovation.

Starting From Within

"Innovate from within" isn't just a catchy phrase; it's a belief system. Before disrupting external boundaries, our internal framework must be in order. Authentic innovation flourishes when our inner beliefs harmonise with desirability, feasibility, and viability.

Diving into these principles: Is It Desired? Desirability scrutinises the relevance of the innovation. A product might be revolutionary, but does it meet an existing market demand? True innovation addresses authentic consumer needs rather than pursuing fleeting trends. Will It Stand Out? In an arena teeming with competitors, feasibility is crucial. It's not merely about inventing but inventing with distinction. What sets your innovation apart? Ensuring a unique value proposition in a sea of offerings sets the stage for lasting success. Is It Sustainable? Viability is the pragmatic side of innovation. Beyond the product's novelty, the numbers need to add up. Can the potential returns cover the expenses of development? Innovation demands risk, but those risks should be well-considered and rooted in strategic financial insight.

Genuine innovation mandates an inward exploration before outward expansion. It's grounded on desirability, feasibility, and viability, and we must perpetually recalibrate, ensuring each move aligns with these guiding principles.

◆ ◆ ◆

The Power Of Starting Small

In times like these, when instant results reign supreme, the wisdom of "starting small" often gets overshadowed. Though simple, this principle bears deep significance.

The saying, "Don't try to boil the ocean," embodies this perfectly. While vast, immediate transformations are tempting, initiating such expansive shifts poses multiple challenges. As in many life pursuits, diving too deep too soon in digital adaptation can strain resources, time, and energy.

Contrary to popular belief, taking things slow isn't stagnation; it's strategic. It ensures that each step is deliberate, informed, and sustainable. Sometimes, this approach can yield faster, lasting results in the end. The early stages of introducing new strategies or methodologies are learning curves. They offer insights into what works and what doesn't.

But, if an organisation takes on too many changes at once, isolating the impact of each becomes overwhelming. It's vital to identify and comprehend what genuinely made a difference.

Addressing one challenge at a time in the digital transformation journey ensures the organisational 'aircraft' remains steady and operational.

The urge for all-encompassing overhauls will be strong. Yet, the thriving transformations will recognise the essence of gradual progress. They'll champion starting small, continuous learning, and informed decision-making. Because the goal isn't just change, it's *meaningful* and *effective* change.

◆ ◆ ◆

The Key To Successful Transformations

We hear stories of unparalleled triumphs all the time. But often hidden beneath these tales are accounts of big and small failures. Ironically, these very setbacks often set the stage for monumental successes. In the digital and organisational transformation context, this concept is encapsulated by the phrase: "Fail Fast."

This notion is more than just a slogan; it's a strategy. It implies that while failure is a given, it can act as a guidepost, highlighting what's effective and what's not.

Instead of taking massive leaps in hopes of immediate transformation, it's about making iterative, smaller adjustments, gauging their effectiveness, and then recalibrating accordingly. Think of it as a system of trial and error: taking incremental steps, assessing their impact, and pivoting as needed.

Nevertheless, while the transformation journey is filled with experimentation and unavoidable setbacks, a clear roadmap is vital. This underscores the need for a coherent set of guiding principles and a clear vision of the intended outcomes. Transformation isn't a straight path. It's more like a roller coaster ride with thrilling peaks and challenging troughs.

And this is where the power of foundational principles comes into play. These principles stand tall as guiding lights throughout all the chaos and confusion. They serve as a consistent reference, helping us revisit and recalibrate our direction, keeping us anchored to our core objectives.

Whether digital or otherwise, transformation is as much about the voyage as it is about the endpoint. It revolves around the bravery to view failures not as hindrances but as opportunities.

Bridging The Divide

"Break down your silos" is a familiar refrain in corporate circles. Yet, how often do we contemplate its depth? Silos, by their very design, compartmentalise - storing grain, data, or in the business context, ideas and expertise. However, in an era celebrating agility and teamwork, these figurative silos obstruct idea flows, causing delays and misunderstandings. The solution isn't mere acknowledgement but proactive dismantling.

Consider an idea's lifecycle. From its inception, as it matures and finds purpose, it faces its initial hurdles often during the design stage. Questions arise: Is our plan comprehensive? How aligned is it with technical capabilities? And by the development phase, do prior decisions get revisited or even discarded?

To truly innovate and craft user-centric products, we must recalibrate our strategies. Here's a roadmap:

- Flow Analysis: Chart the idea's journey. Identify bottlenecks, points of resistance, or redundancy.
- Accountability Tracking: Ensure every stage has a steward who champions the idea's essence.
- Time Audit: In a fast-paced world, every second counts. How long is an idea stationed at each stage? Identify and address delays.
- Collaborative Mindset: Cultivate an environment that emphasises teamwork over mere handovers. Advocate open dialogues that focus on opportunities.
- Gap Bridging: Spot process overlaps or voids. Optimise them for smooth transitions.

But a groundbreaking idea is just the start. Its journey, the collective efforts it garners, and the hurdles it navigates shape its success.

◆ ◆ ◆

Accountability In Product Development

The currents of responsibility can easily be lost amidst a sea of tasks and roles. Without a solid anchor of ownership, even the most potential-laden features risk drifting into the abyss. This scattered sense of responsibility can lead to a vortex of blame, sidetracking organisations from success.

The antidote? Solidify ownership. Entrust someone for every product element. This person oversees the development and ensures that everything aligns from birth to launch and that any discrepancies are swiftly handled.

But simply naming someone isn't the magic bullet. For these stewards to truly excel, they need the right environment. This involves granting them decision-making power, equipping them with needed resources, and nurturing a culture that values their sense of ownership.

To sum up, genuine accountability goes beyond mere delegation; it thrives on empowerment. It's about cultivating a workspace where taking charge is a privilege, not a chore. Where Product professionals not only guide but advocate for their features. By doing so, organisations can shift from a blame-game culture to one celebrating shared triumphs, giving every idea its chance of success.

The Alchemy Of Thought

Nothing wields as profound an influence as our mindset. It is the invisible hand guiding our reactions, shaping our judgments, and determining the paths we choose to follow.

Our psychological landscape is coloured by two contrasting mindsets, the Fixed and the Growth. Each brings a distinctive set of beliefs, reactions, and outcomes.

The Fixed Mindset: The Comfort of Stasis

Those who harbour a fixed mindset see the world through a rather limiting lens. They perceive their abilities and intelligence as static, unchangeable attributes. Challenges become threats, not opportunities. When confronted with obstacles, they're more likely to retreat than to persevere. Criticism is a source of defence rather than an avenue for growth. Such a mindset often finds solace in the familiar, avoiding the unfamiliar terrains that demand adaptation and evolution.

The Growth Mindset: The Odyssey of Evolution

On the other side of the spectrum lies the growth mindset, a perspective rooted in the belief that potential is malleable. Individuals with this mindset approach challenge with zest, seeing them as chances to learn and expand. They view effort not as a testament to their inadequacies but as a bridge to mastery. Criticisms transform into constructive feedback, and the success of others isn't a threat but an inspiration. In their eyes, the world is a playground of endless possibilities, each obstacle an opportunity, each failure a lesson.

The divergence between these two mindsets is not just philosophical, it's transformative. Those with a fixed mindset might find themselves trapped in the confines of their self-imposed limitations. In contrast, individuals with a growth mindset continually evolve, pushing boundaries and turning life into a ceaseless journey of discovery.

Yet, the most empowering truth is this: our mindset is not an immutable trait but a choice. We have the power to decide how we perceive challenges, react to failures, and engage with the world around us. By consciously fostering a growth mindset, we can pave the way for personal and professional success and a life of unbridled learning and fulfilment.

Our destiny isn't written in the stars but crafted by the contours of our mindset. In the grand theatre of life, our mindset is both the script and the director.

Emotional Intelligence

We often become entangled in the race for intellectual excellence, celebrating IQ as the zenith of human potential. Yet, lurking in the shadows of this cerebral marathon is a silent, potent force, Emotional Intelligence, or EQ. It's the unsung hero of human capabilities.

Emotional Intelligence begins with a journey inward. It involves delving deep into our psyche, recognising, and naming our emotions. By understanding our feelings, we not only gain clarity about our motivations but also develop an acute sensitivity to the emotional currents of others. This ability to discern and differentiate between emotions equips us with a richer palette for decision-making. We no longer view situations in black and white but appreciate the multiple hues of human emotion that bring colour to every scenario.

EQ transcends mere recognition; it equips us with the prowess to modulate our emotional responses. Imagine being able to calibrate our emotions, tuning them to resonate with different scenarios or towards the achievement of specific objectives. Someone with high EQ can navigate a storm of anger with the serenity of a sailor or inject optimism into a room clouded with discouragement. This emotional agility enhances personal well-being and fosters environments conducive to collaboration and innovation.

At the heart of Emotional Intelligence lies the magic of human connection. EQ is the compass that guides us through the labyrinth of human relationships, enabling interactions that are both professional and profoundly empathetic. It transforms relationships from mere transactions into meaningful connections. With high EQ, one can sense unspoken sentiments, defuse tensions, and build bridges even when faced with seemingly insurmountable emotional walls.

While our IQ might carve out the path of our academic and professional achievements, it's our EQ that determines the depth and quality of our human experiences. Emotional Intelligence emerges as the thread that binds us to others and anchors us to our very essence.

In celebrating EQ, we acknowledge that being truly human is not just about how smart we are but how deeply we feel, how gracefully we navigate our emotions, and how beautifully we connect with the world around us.

The Power Of True Communication

Communication guides the harmonious interplay of emotions, ideas, and aspirations.

The Greek philosopher Epictetus noted that "we have two ears and one mouth so that we can listen twice as much as we speak". Often mistaken for emptiness, silence is the fertile ground where true understanding sprouts.

As per Stephen Levinson of the Max Planck Institute for Psycholinguistics, the rush to fill conversational voids, a mere 200 milliseconds, often leaves us preparing our responses even as the other speaks. This hasty impulse shadows our innate human ability to genuinely listen.

The Japanese practice of intentional silence, born out of deep respect, serves as a good lesson. By allowing words to truly sink into our consciousness, we elevate the conversation's quality, enriching it with depth and nuance.

Being truly "here and now" roots us in the moment, sharpening our awareness and elevating the clarity of our thoughts. This mindfulness offers the exquisite gift of choice. How to perceive, process, and respond. After expressing ourselves, it is imperative to anchor our attention to our conversational counterpart. Not merely out of politeness but out of genuine curiosity. Within the folds of every perspective lies an opportunity for enlightenment and evolution.

Probing with open-ended inquiries offers a doorway to deeper insights. It beckons the respondent to journey inward, mining for thoughts that transcend superficial layers. Assuming, or even pretending, can tarnish the purity of a conversation. Embracing vulnerability by admitting the unknown can often illuminate the path forward.

The magic of communication lies in its balance. A true conversation is not a monologue but a duet, a melding of voices that enriches both participants. In the end, the power of communication transcends mere words. It is the essence of human connection, the bridge between souls. In each dialogue lies the promise of discovery, growth, and understanding. So, rather than just wielding the instrument of speech, become the mindful architect of your words, forging connections that resonate, inspire, and endure.

Passion And Purpose

As we draw the curtains, I find myself reflecting not just on the vast realm of Product Management but also on the profound journey of human potential. At its core, this book has been a testament to the transformative power that passion, purpose, and persistence hold.

Each chapter, each insight, and each story was carefully crafted to illuminate the path for those who dare to dream, to create, and to make a mark in the ever-evolving world of product development.

But beyond the nuances of product development, strategies, and market dynamics lies a deeper truth, the timeless essence of the human spirit. Our capacity to imagine, adapt, overcome, and excel is what makes us unique.

As you close this book, remember that it is not just about becoming a stellar product professional; it's about embracing the journey with all its highs and lows, its uncertainties and revelations.

Throughout my life, I've learned that true fulfilment doesn't come from achieving a title or mastering a skill. It emanates from the burning desire to contribute, learn, and grow. To truly resonate with the world around us and, in doing so, discover the infinite universe within.

As you move forward, I urge you, dear reader, to view every challenge as an opportunity, every setback as a lesson, and every success as a reminder of what's possible.

Let the tales and insights from this book not just be mere words on paper but seeds that sprout in your heart and mind, guiding you towards a future bursting with innovation, impact, and inspiration.

And always remember: the magic lies not in reaching the destination but in savouring the journey. The roads less travelled, the mountains scaled, the rivers crossed, they shape us, mould us, and ultimately, define us. Dive into your journey with an open heart, a curious mind, and the unwavering belief that the universe conspires in favour of those who dare to dream.

May your passion be your compass and your purpose, your North Star. And when in doubt, remember that you hold within you the power to change the world, one product, one idea, one heartbeat at a time.

AFTERWORD

"*My journey has taken me through the dynamic world of business and the intricate realm of digital creation. I'm driven by a genuine desire to craft digital solutions that resonate globally and make daily life richer and more seamless.*

Beyond my work, I take pride in guiding emerging talents and sharing insights with peers through writing. This book? It's a reflection of my passion, my growth, and my commitment to fostering a culture of continuous learning and innovation.

As you've turned its pages, hopefully, you will have discovered actionable insights and strategies, ensuring that you, too, can embark on a transformative journey in the Product realm.

Here's to the magic that awaits. Here's to you."

Andrei Adam